Catholic Social Teaching

Catholic Social Teaching

A textbook of Christian insights

by

Theodor Herr

with an introduction

by

Rodger Charles S.J.

New City
London   Edinburgh   Dublin

First published in Germany
as
Katholische Soziallehre
by
Verlag Bonfatius-Druckerei Paderborn
© 1987 Verlag Bonfatius-Druckerei Paderborn

First Published in Great Britain 1991
by
New City
57 Twyford Avenue, London W3 9PZ

Translated by Pieter Vlieland
© English translation New City 1991

**A catalogue record for this book is available
from the British Library**

ISBN 0 904287 40 8

Typeset in Great Britain
by
Chippendale Type Ltd., Otley, West Yorkshire
Printed and bound in Great Britain
by
Billing and Sons Ltd., Worcester

Contents

Part Three

General Introduction

by

Rodger Charles S.J.

I. Catholic social teaching in the 1980's and 1990's

In recommending Theodor Herr's book to an English readership, and doing so with enthusiasm, I must admit that when I was first looking over it I had some doubts whether I would be able to so recommend it; fuller acquaintance with it, however, banished them. As I digested it more fully it was clear that it represented a useful addition to the all too limited serious literature on the subject and the publishers, New City, deserve our thanks for making it available more widely.

The reasons for my initial reservations, however, may have bearing for other potential readers and I think it will be useful to state them, and to show why despite them I am enthusiastic. They will also provide a preamble to comments I wish to make on parts of the text. There were two main such reservations. First of all, the question of whether a textbook written for the German context, and with so many of its topical references being to that context, was suitable for an English market. Secondly, if it was suitable in its general contents, was it suitable in detail, given that no major rewriting of a study first published five years ago and growing out of a series of articles planned in 1983 was intended?

The first problem was not a major one. Some adjustments were to be made, and while there are still passages which directly refer to the German experience, they deal with points of principle or procedure which have wider application. The second problem was more difficult. Much has been happening in the field of Catholic social teaching in the last few years as John Paul II has got into his stride, reviving interest in the subject as he faced some of the basic questions that had led to its being overshadowed a while from the late 1960's. We have had the two documents from the Congregation for the Doctrine of the Faith on liberation theology, *Libertatis Nuntius*[1] (1984) and *Libertatis Conscientia* (1986) and John Paul II's *Message to the Brazilian Church* (also 1986), followed by another social encyclical *Sollicitudo Rei Socialis* (1987). While the first two of these are used briefly in the documentation, the text would have been much improved if their overall insights had been used more fully, and the encyclical is not dealt with at all. This brings us to another problem: the book does not look at the Church's teaching on the relations between the developed and underdeveloped countries, which was what the encyclical was about.

Not only were there important developments in the teaching in this period, but there has also been the most dramatic turn of events in Eastern Europe and Soviet Russia which very directly affects aspects of, or understanding of, the social magisterium. The rejection of Marxism in these countries confirmed the Church's insistence from the beginning that Marxism was in error in its comprehension of humanity and its needs. Some still hope that the true Marxism, which they claim has not yet been tried, may yet be vindicated; but at the moment it looks as if it has been tried and found wanting. Certainly the Church's rejection of forms of liberation theology which had pinned their hope to the validity of Marxist social analysis and the achievements of Soviet Marxism has been vindicated.

The end of the 1980's into the 1990's, therefore, presents a very different picture of the Church's relationship with the world and consequently of the relevance of her social ethics, from the one presented in the early and middle 1980's. Then the Church was very much on the defensive as it seemed that the social teaching, and her role in these matters as 'mother and teacher of the nations' in John XXIII's enthusiastic words, was limited if not finished. As the decade went on this became less and less the case, and given that Professor Herr's work would have been a somewhat different one if written at any time in the last four years, the question was, was it absolutely necesssary to have more than the few changes incorporated since 1987?

I decided that it was not, because the body of the book, its essential content, is of enduring value and as such, as I said at the beginning, it represents a very useful contribution to the sparse serious literature there is on the subject in English. It will help considerably in the study and proper understanding of Catholic social teaching, for it provides a really solid question and answer introduction to its subject.

Regarding its major omission, that it does not deal with the Church's teaching on the relationship between the developed and underdeveloped countries: the principles on which the Church approaches the question of justice between these nations are the same as those regulating justice between persons and groups of persons, and they are dealt with in these pages. The fundamental principle is the dignity the human person possesses in being made in God's image and redeemed by his son Jesus Christ. Since all possess this dignity, all have a natural right to a life worthy of it.

Solidarity with others is a consequence of this principle and it has implications, for example, in terms of international relations on political and economic matters. These, especially where they concern the underdeveloped countries, are to be based on justice and charity. At the same time, these countries themselves have the prime responsibility for their development, which requires honest and efficient government, that they build on the natural talents of the people and that they consider first the needs of basic development rather than prestige projects. In practice the disparities in wealth between the rich nations and poor, the latter lacking the necessities of a decent life, the former plagued by consumerism, show clearly how God's gift of the world to all that all might enjoy a good life from it is not being used correctly. *Gaudium et Spes, Populorum Progressio* and *Sollicitudo Rei Socialis* give us guidance on why this is so and moral lines for a solution.

II. Lessons to be learned from the eclipse of the social teaching of the Church in the 1960's and 1970's.

One of the main reasons why this volume will help the serious study and the proper understanding of the social teaching of the Church is because it does not disguise the difficulties of the subject, often underestimated, but at the same time it leads the patient reader through those difficulties to a profounder understanding of that teaching. It is this combination of characteristics that is one of the requirements for improving the quality of teaching of the subject.

For I think it is important for all those concerned with education in this field to realize that there are lessons to be learned from the collapse of confidence in the Church's social teaching which occurred in the wake of the Council. It would seem that the general answer to the question of why that collapse of confidence took place lies in the attitudes of the late 1960's, when there was a comprehensive questioning of many aspects of Christian culture which survived in the capitalist democracies. Unfortunately, in this atmosphere, the necessary developments in liturgy, teaching and discipline that were made through the Vatican Council in order to equip the Church better to meet the needs of the late 20th century and beyond were easily misinterpreted to mean that any change that took the popular fancy was justifiable without reference to tradition or magisterium. Hence the careful words of the social encyclicals and of the Council itself were too readily dismissed as irrelevant.

Further, the encyclicals could be narrowly interpreted so as to appear to confirm such an approach. For example, John XXIII's *Pacem in Terris* (159 to 160) distinguished between erroneous social philosophies and the policies based on them, and said that these policies might be such as to make it possible and desirable to work with those responsible for their application. Taken out of context this could be made to mean that the theoretical differences did not matter either, or even that the false philosophies were no longer false but true. The fuller context denied that possibility, however, by adding that all such co-operation should 'respect the natural law, the social teaching of the Church and the directives of ecclesiastical authority'.

Octogesima Adveniens noted it was difficult for the Church 'to put forward a solution which has universal validity' (4); out of context this could be taken to mean that there was no longer a coherent social doctrine, but the context excluded this interpretation since it continued by saying that the gospel and the social teaching of the Church will give 'principles for reflection, norms of judgement and guidelines for action'.

Paul VI just stated in sharper terms the Church's insistence already clearly laid out for example in *Quadragesimo Anno* (41) and *Gaudium et Spes* (42, 76) that she had no solution or particular set of solutions to the political and economic problems of every different society in their ever changing circumstances. Finding these is the task of the experts in those fields and putting them into practice is the job of properly constituted political authority. The Christian has the means of knowing, through the Church's social teaching, what the morally acceptable options are and on that basis decides his or her own personal allegiance.

As one who has been seeking ways of maintaining the tradition in the years since the Council, without having had any personal knowledge or direct experience of its former flourishing, I remember very distinctly the reaction of some of those who had at one time been impressed by the teaching and had become disillusioned by the 1960's, and I remember too the reasons given for that disillusionment. Almost invariably, it was that they had misunderstood what the teaching was about, and in consequence they had been lead to expect more of it than it was intended to or could give them. In particular they had looked to it for instant wisdom on the thorniest of theoretical and practical, political and economic problems of the moment, and finding it wanting in this had abandoned it and regarded anyone who took it seriously as, at best, somewhat naïve.

They had expected, in other words, that the documents published for the moral guidance of the whole Church would be more expert on the specific answers, policies, prescriptions applicable to a particular country at an exact point in time, than the practical and theoretical wisdom of the experts of that country in the fields concerned, and, likewise, that the documents would be more adept at spotting the best immediate political options than the professionals themselves. Not surprisingly they were disappointed.

As the brief passage from *Octogesima Adveniens* indicates, the social teaching of the Church is not of that sort. As part of her moral theology it gives guidance to the practical judgement, not on political and economic systems and policies, but on the moral values that these should respect if they are to be worthy of human dignity. It is then entirely practical, as indeed the whole of moral theology is a practical science not a speculative one. Catholic social teaching establishes moral values, which, in terms of practical politics and economics, can usually be served by taking any one of several courses according to one's reading of the situation.

We, the individual citizens of individual countries, lay and clerical, have the duty of making up our minds, guided by these values, on these practical issues and using our power as citizens to help towards their solution. The basic power all have in a free society is that of the ballot box. What other active commitment we take is up to us according to our responsibilities and opportunities, though there is, of course, a basic difference between the responsibilities of laity and clergy in this matter.

The exact relationship of clergy and laity concerning the social apostolate has been the cause of much controversy in recent years. The truth is that the laity have the primary responsibility and privilege of active involvement in partisan politics, and in organized economic and social action in the various branches of civil life (GS 43, AA 4). In other words they have an opportunity to sanctify the world through their Christian commitment which is denied to the clergy. The role of the Church is educative, exhortatory and supportive, and the clergy are not to identify publicly with partisan or purely secular causes,[2] though they too are entitled to their personal political convictions and must exercise their basic responsibilities here. If it should be necessary for the Church to identify a politically sensitive issue on which she must speak, because the good of souls or human rights are involved, then it is for the Bishops to decide and to decide with the good not only of the national Church in mind but that of the whole Church.

Had these two things, the exact nature of the Church's claim for her social teaching, and the different roles of the laity and the clergy in the sanctification of the world through the civil order, been properly understood and clearly taught, I do not think that the disillusion I spoke of would have occurred. The teaching is a moral teaching, an ethical teaching, and the responsibility for applying it in practice is an individual responsibility which we exercise by making our commitment through the normal means that society offers us to participate in public life. There is no Catholic economics, politics or social system as such. Nor should the laity expect the hierarchical Church or its ministers to take the initiative in partisan politics. Her concern is with human rights and the good of souls. There are grey areas here of course, and there will always be tensions between Church and state in practice, but there should not be sustained misunderstanding in principle, leading to destructive division in the Church.

In this context, the value of a book like this is that, while it does not have the time or the space to deal with all aspects of the teaching, it deals with the essentials and it does so in a way which prevents over simplification. Its question and answer form is calculated to highlight problems while encouraging the progress to intelligent, thoughtful answers which should provide a sound basis for further enquiry, understanding and action.

The three major sections deal with firstly, basic questions in Catholic social teaching, secondly, the economic and social order from a Christian point of view and thirdly, Christ and politics, Church and state. It is an arrangement which, combined with the question and answer method, enables most of the major issues that arise in understanding the teaching to be teased out. The methodology has the vices of its virtues, in that none of the areas of teaching is laid out positively and comprehensively, although the documentation after each of the 40 or so sections does something to this end by presenting relevant extracts from Church documents on the points in question. Yet the advantages far outweigh the disadvantages in terms of sound pedagogy in this introductory study. The key points are brought out and the questions they in their turn raise, stimulate further enquiry, while the subject is not deadened at the outset with too much theoretical and historical structuring.

III. Commentary on Part One: Basic Questions

The first part explores such questions as the authority of the Church on social matters, the sources of her social teaching, and the phenomena of political theology and political liberation. Concepts basic to Christian thinking about humanity and society are also examined, for example, personal dignity and work, solidarity and subsidiarity, justice and charity, the common good, and our responsibility for God's creation.

The method then means that each of these subjects can only be analysed briefly and inevitably there are gaps and foreshortened comments. What is said on the relationship of the modern social teaching to the scriptures, for example, does not seem to me to be as coherent as it might be. I doubt if the Sermon on the Mount should really be a problem in terms of social ethics. The sermon is concerned with the inner nature of Christian morality and spirituality. It does not mean that he who has care of the common good must cease to do justice, which includes curbing the wrong-doer if necessary by force, for this is part of his moral responsibility towards society. It does mean that justice should not be done in a spirit of vengeance or contempt for the evil-doer and that only that degree and kind of force is used which is compatible with the human dignity of the offender and is necessary to protect the common weal.

The question of liberation theology needs further clarification too, and this is where a fuller appropriation of *Libertatis Conscientia* and John Paul II's teaching would have been of value. Liberation theology has now been accepted as a valid term, and I think a crucial one in Catholic theology and this has considerable importance for the Church's social teaching. In his *Message to the Brazilian Church* in 1986, John Paul II said that the theology of liberation was 'not only opportune but useful and necessary' but that of its nature such theology is primarily soteriological, i.e., salvational, 'an aspect of the salvation won for us by Jesus Christ . . . and only secondarily to do with social ethics [or political ethics]'. It cannot therefore be reduced to the socio-ethical aspects, for the latter are a consequence of the soteriological (LC 71).

Yet what is important in the context of the development of Catholic social teaching is that the message of salvation has this consequence. Christ saved us and set us free from self-love which is the source of injustice but we must persevere and not fall victim to that self-love again (LC53). The first liberation must be through conversion, but at the same time, where unjust structures do oppress the poor it is legitimate for us to seek to change them and get better justice, provided methods compatible with the gospel are used (LC 75). The myth of revolution as a general means to that end, while despising the path of reform, is to be rejected (LC 78), although in certain extreme cases and as a last resort armed struggle might be justified (LC 79).

What is so important about all this is the assertion that liberation *is primarily soteriological and only secondarily socio-ethical*, with the social teaching of the Church being the social ethics of liberation theology (LC Ch. V). This does two things.

In the first place, it makes it impossible any longer to claim that concern with justice in social, political and economic matters is not an essential part of the Christian vocation of all but simply the personal interest of a few. On the contrary, if we accept that to be a Christian is to try to remain free of self-love, we must fight that self-love that would deny charity and justice to others in society. The first stage is to change attitudes in ourselves and others, but we must also seek to change the structures that encourage injustice.

In the second place, it undermines the position of those who would seek a social ethic at variance with the Christian view of humanity and of relationships within society. The Christian social, political and economic ethics, the Church's social teaching is the guide to true Christian liberation. Liberation theology therefore, if we properly understand the concept, frees the Church from the twin forces which always threaten to tear her apart over these matters. It rejects the common objection of the extreme right wing social and political lobby of the Church, that she should keep her nose out of these world matters and leave them to men of property and business. On the other hand, it also rejects the extreme left wing view that has tried to get the Church committed to class warfare in the Marxist sense and to the illusion that the social ownership of productive goods is the path to economic well-being. This still leaves us free to choose a political commitment in any of the main groups in democratic society, since all embrace a wide range of views compatible with Catholic social teaching.

IV. Commentary on Part Two: Economics and Economic Order from the Christian Point of View

The second section deals with long-standing controversies that are familiar to all students of Catholic social ethics, though liberation theology is touched on once again. Some might think that the emphasis on the defects of modern trade unionism are stressed a little too much, but there is room for differences of opinion here and what is said is well within them. Overall the full Catholic teaching on the rights of labour is given generous treatment along with the full teaching also on the rights of capitalism in the Christian understanding of that word.

The sort of questions that are asked in this section, about capitalism, Christianity and the social market for example, have recently been looked at with new clarity and force in *Centesimus Annus*. The new interest in capitalism as an alternative to the real socialism that has failed in Eastern Europe has made guidance on this issue very timely.

First of all, the encyclical contrasts various forms of the free market economy. One was the social market, with a sound currency and social stability providing the conditions for steady growth, so that the people could work to build a better future for themselves and their families. It also embodied respect for the social responsibilities of private ownership ensured by public watchfulness that prevents the market mechanism being the only criterion of the social good, established the goals of securing high employment levels, social security, adequate professional training, the right of association in free trade unions, and democratic participation which prevents the worker being degraded by reducing labour to a mere commodity (CA 19). The social market was an attempt to rebuild democracy on the basis of social justice.

By contrast some 'national security' states have been so paralysed by fear of communism that they have denied their people basic freedoms. Another equal error has been that of the pursuit of affluence for its own sake, extolling the advantages of the market in purely materialistic terms, excluding spiritual and cultural values, morality, law and religion from consideration, and becoming as materialist as Marxism (CA 19). The free market in these senses is clearly not acceptable.

The importance given to private property, understood in the perspective of the universal destination of material goods, however, is acceptable. Hence so too is the contribution of the entrepreneur, defined in a way that fits the role to the needs of morality as 'the person who produces something . . . in order that others may use it after they have paid a just price through free bargaining'. It is precisely 'the ability to foresee both the needs of others and the combination of productive factors most adapted to satisfying those needs which constitute another important source of wealth in modern society' (CA 32).

The role of private ownership of productive goods as the engine of a healthy economy has always been implicit in the Church's defence of them. She is well aware that it is the possibility of working those goods for profit which has always interested their owners. Particularly in the high middle ages, when modern capitalism was born, this was the case.

Her moral theologians were familiar with the realities of practical economics in the market place. It is one of them, St Antoninus of Florence that Schumpeter[3] gives the credit of perhaps first conceiving of the economic process as a whole. Cases of conscience over the market economy, the selling of goods at a profit and the taking of interest on loans, were the heart of the moralists' concerns and gave them a considerable understanding of the working of the market. Nor did their presence seriously hinder its working, indeed it is said to have had a positive formative influence on it.[4] It is now generally recognized that the moralists were much more sophisticated in their appreciation of market forces than was at one time thought, though they were never naïve enough to think that they formed an independent and automatically functioning moral system in their own right. It was left to the Enlightenment to come to that conclusion.

That human freedom, creativity and responsibility were manifest in the private ownership of productive goods when it is exercised in accordance with the moral law, is the reason the Church has always defended it. That it should also be the basis of a healthy economy is what one might expect, since it is persons who operate the economy and if they are allowed the full exercise of their creativity and responsibility in doing so, the economy should work well.

There are important provisos attached, however. The first is that many, perhaps the majority throughout the world today do not have the opportunity to make a creative contribution to a modern national economy. Their marginalization is a great injustice. The second is that the ruthlessness of the capitalist who does not accept the limitations of morality on his actions breaks out when given the chance, and many capitalists do not accept those limits. There are enough examples in the developed, as well as in the underdeveloped world, to confirm this (CA 33). The third is that there are many human needs which are not relevant to the market, because no one would be interested in providing for them at a price the needy could afford. If the needs are such that those who are in want can be helped to become independent by entering the market system, this is the best answer. If this cannot be done then it must be remembered that human needs and human rights are prior to the market (CA 34).

In this context, the role of the unions in seeing justice is done is valid. It is a society of free work, of enterprise and participation that the Church defends, and the forces of society and the state must see that this justice is done (CA 35). Profit that is made by a business in a free market and in ways that respect the rights of its employees indicates that the business is functioning properly; the profit then is justified because it has matched human need and available resources in a way which serves the customer and society at large. We may not assume, however, that since real socialism has failed, capitalism as we know it is necessarily the answer (CA 35) from a Christian point of view.

Capitalism, in the sense of an economic system that 'accepts the fundamental and positive role of business, the market, private property and responsibility for the means of production and free human creativity in the economic sector', is acceptable (CA 42), though it is probably better to call it a free economy. Capitalism which is above the law and sees the market and competition as a form of economic morality without reference to spiritual or cultural needs, justice, law or objective morals is by the same token rejected (CA 42).

Doubts about the morality of Western capitalism at the moment arise firstly from its treatment of the third world. It must offer that world better opportunities of participating in the development process, while the countries concerned themselves have the duty of organizing their internal affairs soundly and justly (CA 35).

They arise also from its consumerism. Having reached the stage where the means of satisfying basic needs are for the vast majority easily available, the danger is that seeking satisfaction of inessential, artificial or even anti-social or immoral needs will become an end in itself. 'Of itself an economic system does not possess criteria for correctly distinguishing new and higher forms of satisfying human needs from artificial new needs which hinder the formation of a mature personality' (CA 36). Educational and cultural work is needed to help in the responsible use of choice.

Drugs and pornography are evidence of consumerism at its worst. Of course, it is not wrong to want to live better; but it is wrong to want more simply to make enjoyment of things an end in itself without reference to truth, goodness, beauty, and the needs of others (CA 36). It also tends to destruction of the balance of nature around us, because a consumerist mentality exploits the environment without regard to real need (CA 37). Human ecology is also at risk through neglect of proper planning in urbanization, for example (CA38), through the undermining of the family by denigrating stable marriage and its role as the sanctuary of life (CA 39), reducing children to 'things' according to taste, and destroying life at its source through abortion.

Just as in the old capitalism the state had to interfere to protect the rights of the workers through factory legislation and the rest, in the new there are collective and qualitative needs that the market cannot meet. The market can be made the object of idolatry (CA 40). Marx was wrong about the nature and cause of the alienation that afflicted capitalist society, but alienation in it there is, alienation from true personhood by over concentration on material goods. Man cannot be content with the false utopia of material gratification; if he refuses to admit his transcendence through self-giving and authentic human community, he is alienated from his true self (CA 41).

V. Commentary on Part Three: Church and State

The third section, on Church and state, deals with some of the historical questions that have helped form the mind of the Church on this matter. Here again we see a particular merit of the book: that it gives the reader some idea of the complexity of the issues and the depth of the Church's experience in dealing with them, and this is especially important in this area. I shall consider here a few points which the text was not able to discuss, or deals with only briefly, and which seem to me crucial.

There are certainly two strands in the Catholic tradition concerning theories about the origin and purpose of the state, but they are not of equal authority overall. According to the Fathers of the Church, who were concerned only with political theory in passing, the state was the result of the Fall of man and its main purpose is coercive; it exists to impose limits on the transgressions of man that flow from his wounded nature.[5]

St Thomas, however, wrote at a time when the Catholic tradition was coming to maturity and its political ethics were more developed, especially through the insights provided by Aristotle's political thought. For St Thomas, therefore, the state was in accordance with man's nature before the Fall and it meets the needs of that nature in the best sense, perfecting him, giving him a full life;[6] this positive view of the state as natural to man became the accepted teaching (GS 74). It better represents the more balanced view of an institution, the state, whose authority is guaranteed by God and whose nature is founded in the natural law in the Thomistic sense which, again, the Church has made her own.

St Augustine saw that man was by nature a social being, but he did not see that the state and its authority were natural: to him both were the results of sin.[7] For Thomas the relationship of ruler and ruled would have existed before the Fall.[8] Man was not only a social being, naturally drawn to live in society with others, but he was a social-political being, one to whom the state, and the authority that was a requisite of such a society, was natural.

This teaching of the Church's *Doctor Communis* shows that the Church's tradition here has developed very positively in its appreciation of the state and the political order. It did so by drawing on the political theory and experience of the Middle Ages which, according to the Carlyles,[9] bore the following characteristics: it made justice the end of political society; it made law the norm of that justice and by which all, including the ruler, were to be judged; and it made the notion of contract the basis of the relationship between ruler and ruled with the implicit right to break that relationship if the terms were not kept. In addition, representative government was evolving generally throughout Europe from the late 13th century against the background of these ideas. When we reflect on this, we wonder at the waywardness of European political thought and practice from the Renaissance to Rousseau.

The mass of historical data this short section had to draw on meant that much had to be omitted. The later medieval and early modern scholastic view of the forms of state and the origins of political authority are worth recalling. They are best expressed by St Thomas in the *Summa*: the best form of polity is one in which the people choose their rulers and rulers can be chosen from among the people.[10] It was then a theory of popular sovereignty, political power coming ultimately from God, but from him through the people and not directly to the ruler. The same theory was held and elaborated by Suarez and Bellarmine,[11] the latter being in controversy with James I of England and VI of Scotland on the question of absolutism and divine right.

The solid Catholic philosophical and theological tradition in its maturity was for popular sovereignty, although the older divine right theory had its advocates. The circumstances which identified the Church with absolute monarchy were: the post-reformation political and ecclesiastical situation in Europe which marginalized her; the excesses of the French revolution which demonstrated the evils of totalitarian democracy; and the difficulties, in the 19th century, of the Papacy which was faced with the threat of the loss of temporal power with no practical alternative in sight that would guarantee its necessary political independence. Yet, as Leo XIII pointed out long before he or his immediate successors were sure modern representative democracy could be positively recommended, the teaching was that people have a right to choose whatever form of government suits them,[12] provided only it seeks justice. The reservation about modern democracy was whether, with certain examples in mind, it was capable of fulfilling that proviso.

When *Centesimus Annus*, which also has a great deal to say on the Christian view of the political order, states that modern democracy is valued by the Church because it ensures citizen participation in politics, enables the governed to elect and hold accountable those who govern them, and to replace them by peaceful means when appropriate (CA 46), it reflects a judgement on that democracy which had been increasingly positive since the time of Pius XII (1939 to 1958). Yet the tradition shows that the Church is no stranger to the idea of popular sovereignty. It was the experience of dealing with the totalitarianism of Stalin and Hitler that highlighted the virtues of the stable democracies of Western Europe and North America, and then the struggle against fascism in the Second World War, that finally influenced Pius XII's views. John Paul II is simply summing up the tendency since.

Authentic democracy depends on the rule of law and the acceptance of the dignity of the human person (CA 46). In the light of the collapse of communism, there is new interest in democracy and human rights (CA 47) and care must be taken to understand these correctly. The basic human right is the right to life which is sacred from the moment of conception, and from this follows the right to live in a united family and in a moral environment conducive to full development in freedom and truth, so that in turn the individual persons can accept responsibility for their own destinies in due time, live by these standards and pass them on to their children. These, and the duty of the state to seek the common good, are not necessarily secure in the modern democratic state. The guardianship of the common good can also easily be surrendered in the struggle for power and influence by special interest groups. The constitutional solutions to these problems is not the Church's concern, but for the various peoples themselves to work out. Her only interest is to protect the dignity of the human person revealed in God made man.

In its relationship with the economic life of the people the same rights and freedoms are to be fostered. Respect for honest work that brings due rewards, for private property, economic stability, probity in business and public life provide the right context for freedom and responsibility: the state's role is to provide the institutional, juridical, and political framework which will foster these things (CA 48). In the every day working of the economy the prime responsibility and initiative rests with individuals and groups, not the state, according to the principle of subsidiarity. Yet the state must support those activities and institutions which secure the economic health of the community, especially when they are weakened, without extending state supervision needlessly; poverty and deprivation are to be remedied by social welfare, subject to the principle of subsidiarity (CA 48).

More fundamental social attitudes are to be fostered by the state also, solidarity and charity in particular, because they challenge selfish individualism (CA 49). In particular, the family needs support by wise social policies that assist it with its work within the generations and between them, parents, children, the aged. There are, in other words, social groups apart from those that enable the state and the market to function. Man is not only a political animal, and a producer and consumer of goods, he is above all a seeker after truth and the ways of applying it in daily existence. From this varied life arises a nation's culture, which provides it with a set of accepted values, and which the young will challenge in order to test themselves and find their place in the changing scheme of things (CA 50). Evangelization is part of this culture and sustains it in its search for truth.

Dr Charles is a Jesuit priest on the staff of Campion Hall Oxford where he has a research tutorship in social ethics, and is a member of the University Theology Faculty. His publications include *Christian Ethics and the Problems of Society* (1975) and *The Social Teaching of Vatican II* (1982).

Notes

[1]For the details of the editions of these and other Roman and Papal documents referred to in the text throughout the Introduction, and for the abbreviations used, see the note at the end.

[2]John Paul II *Address to Major Religious Superiors* in Rome November 24th 1978; *Address to Priests and Male Religious* in Mexico, Basilica of Our Lady of Guadalupe, January 27th 1979; *Puebla, Pilgrimage of Faith*, Boston 1979 p. 71.

[3]J.A. Schumpeter, *A History of Economic Analysis*, London 1963 p. 95.

[4]It was the moralists' insistence on the moral binding force of the simple agreement, irrespective of the Roman law tradition in the matter, which was crucial to the business transaction as it developed. 'The ethics of the Church, so strong on this point ensured the development of the free market' *Cambridge Economic History of Europe*, Volume III, CUP 1965 p. 561. On the economic effect of the guilds see Chapter V of the same, on the just price and usury, J. Gilchrist, *The Church and Economic Activity in the Middle Ages*, London 1969.

[5]R.W. and A.J. Carlyle, *A History of Medieval Political Theory in the West*, Vol. 1. London 1903 p. 131.

[6]*De Regimine Principum* (On Kingship) Chapter 1.

[7]Carlyle and Carlyle, op.cit., Vol. 1. p. 126. *St Augustine, De Civitate Dei* XIX 12, 15.

[8]*Summa Theologica* I q. 92 art. 1 ad. 2.

[9]Carlyle and Carlyle, op.cit., Vol. 6 p. 504.

[10]*Summa Theologica* I II q. 105 art. 1

[11]James Broderick SJ, *Blessed Robert Bellarmine*, Vol. 1 London 1928 p. 235; Quentin Skinner, *The Foundations of Modern Political Thought*, Vol. 2 CUP 1978 p. 174.

[12]In the encyclical *Diuturnum Illud* of 1881: 'So long as justice be respected, the people are not hindered from choosing for themselves that form of government which best suits . . . their own disposition' (7).

Documentation and abbreviations

AA   *Apostolicam Actuositatem* (Decree on the Laity), Second Vatican Council 1965, *Vatican Council II* The Conciliar and Post Conciliar Documents, editor A. Flannery OP, Wilmington Del., 1975

CA   *Centesimus Annus*, Encyclical of John Paul II, Vatican Polyglot Press, 1991

GS   *Gaudium et Spes* (Decree on the Church in the Modern World), Second Vatican Council, 1965, in Flannery op.cit.

LC   *Libertatis Conscientia*, Instruction of the Congregation for the Doctrine of the Faith, CTS London

LN   *Libertatis Nuntius*, Instruction of the Congregation for the Doctrine of the Faith, CTS London 1986

OA   *Octogesima Adveniens*, Apostolic Letter of Paul VI, CTS London 1971

Pacem in Terris, Encyclical of John XXIII 1963, CTS London 1965

Quadragesimo Anno, Encyclical of Pius XI 1931 CTS London 1960

Sollicitudo Rei Socialis, Encyclical of John Paul II CTS London 1987

Message to the Church in Brazil, Letter of John Paul II CIIR London 1986

Preface

The various articles in this introduction to Catholic social teaching were published as a continuous series in the Catholic daily *Deutsche Tagespost* of Würzburg between August 1984 and February 1986. The series was first suggested at an editorial conference in the autumn of 1983 and began with a set of articles on general questions and principles, followed by further articles on economics and politics. The publisher was urged by many readers to issue the series in book form: this publication is therefore the response to their wishes.

The original texts have been left largely as they were, with minor changes here and there, and so they bring to a wider public in this form a general introduction to the subject. The alterations are mainly in chapter titles as the original headings had to meet the demands of newspaper publishing. There have also been minor changes to meet the needs of book publishing. Introductory texts intended to make it easier to place in correct order the overall context of Catholic social teaching have also been added, as have quotations from official Church documents which should allow wider consideration of the issues dealt with.

This 'textbook', then, is intended for all those who are interested in the Church's social message. It is not aimed at any special group or section of society. Its first purpose is to give information and inspire broader concern for individual issues and Catholic social teaching as a whole. The language has been kept deliberately simple avoiding scholarly apparatus, so that as many interested people as possible can be reached. In this form the book is also suitable for theology students, giving them their first overview of this subject.

Presentation

Catholic social teaching draws its basic material from two sources: the one general and a matter of principles and the other specific. The general part deals with the foundations of the Church's social message and its theoretical principles. It does not just give practical suggestions but constitutes an academic discipline. In this academic realm social concepts are dealt with, including the family, society, the state, international society etc., as well as social institutions such as property, law, economics, capital, labour, trade unions, associations etc. The specific part can be divided into four related areas: the family, the economy, the state and the community of nations. This 'textbook' will deal in the first place with the basic questions of the general part and, following on from that, with the 'classic' themes of specific social teaching, the economy and the state.

The following subjects will not be considered, even though they should be mentioned for the sake of completeness: the family, international relations or the community of nations, the history of the Catholic social movement, and exegesis, that is, the systematic explanation of the official texts. In Catholic social teaching since the 19th century a special position has been reserved for conflict between competing social systems, in particular capitalism and socialism. While this important issue is not being dealt with in detail in this 'textbook', it has not been neglected. The reader will soon realize that confrontation between the competing systems runs through the articles and the overall treatment like a golden thread. Within the framework of this first analysis of Catholic social teaching it seemed to us that the treatment of the family could be dispensed with, since information in this field is already generally available. Other topics, in particular social history, have been left aside because they would have gone beyond the bounds of an introduction on this scale. The reader is referred to the specialized literature on these complex questions.

In general our subject, Catholic social teaching, is examined as a complete and independent field in which autonomous material is looked at, for which reason we write 'Catholic' with a capital 'C'. This means, for example, that we shall base our examination as far as possible on the Church's social teaching as officially proclaimed and expressed in official documents. We work from the assumption that the Church's social doctrine is more than just the sum of occasional utterances on current social issues. It is certainly true that the Church does not wish to put forward a complete and closed social system. We can even say the system is open-ended. Even so, we are of the opinion that Catholic social teaching at its core presents a complex of pronouncements by the magisterium which builds systematically on the unchangeable foundations of Christian human and social relationships and which, looked at as a whole, can be seen as clearly distinct from other concepts of society.

In the end, systematic understanding and scientific analysis are not a matter for the Church's Magisterium but for Catholic social sciences. Consequently, a distinction has to be drawn in principle between the Church's official social teaching on the one hand and, on the other, Catholic social sciences as taught in the universities. When it comes to the scholarly interpretation of official teachings, particularly in the field of academic research and development, it is natural that there should be different assessments, interpretative models and ways of approach. To go further, we must give special attention to practical social action. On the one hand, this is a matter of translating the Church's social teaching into concrete social and economic policy, while, on the other hand, it is a matter of working with those involved in social relations, that is, with individuals and groups or with the peoples of developing countries.

The individual chapters of this book were, as already explained, published as articles in the *Deutsche Tagespost*. For book publication they have remained unaltered apart from minor extrapolations and corrections. Even so, every chapter has had added to it an introductory text that explains briefly the matters to be dealt with and shows their place in the overall field. In this way the reader who is interested but knows very little beforehand is helped towards a better grasp of the subject. There is also for every chapter a relevant text from official papal or episcopal pronouncements. In the nature of things, pride of place goes to papal encyclicals. According to the matter in hand, other quotations are used which are of particular importance for each article. This enables the reader to gain insight into the official texts and to study the social teaching at source. At the same time, these texts make it possible to use this book for teaching purposes and in group discussions. This, too, was the expressed wish of those who originally read the articles in the newspaper.

PART ONE

Basic questions of Catholic social teaching

This first part deals with something inherent in the teaching of principles, namely, the general or basic part of Catholic social teaching. The subjects dealt with explain clearly what is needed for understanding it and its methods of operation. It should be particularly borne in mind that Catholic social teaching bases its socio-ethical standpoints both on the scriptures, which is to say, on revelation, and on natural justice.

Socio-ethical standards are effective in society only when they are successful in making their good sense and necessity obvious to everybody. Their social acceptability depends on it: without that even the finest social norms would be useless. Catholic social teaching does not only have to produce proof that its social standards and principles accord with the Bible and revelation, it must also have the power to make it clear that the norms, binding in the first instance only on Christians and believers, are also sensible and prudent for everyone else – otherwise they cannot be made binding on the public in a pluralistic society.

It is therefore important for this teaching that it rests not just on the scriptures but also on natural moral law and general human convictions about justice as they have found their expression in Christian natural law. Contrary to opinions occasionally expressed, even after the Second Vatican Council, the Church adheres basically to natural law.

In his encyclical *Laborem Exercens*, Pope John Paul II based the social rights of working people on general natural law, i.e., the rights that arise 'from the nature of man' as 'fundamental rights of the person' (No. 16). It should always be remembered that according to Catholic social teaching there is no basic difference between the two sources of knowledge, between revelation and natural law, 'because in reality the sacred and secular have their origin in the same God' (Pastoral Constitution *Gaudium et Spes*, No. 36).

1. What authority has the Church in economic and social questions?

It is generally considered – not least by itself – that the Church has a mission that is religious and not primarily political. From that it follows that the Church is neither a political nor an economic institution. And so, before the details of the Church's social teaching are examined, it must be made clear whether the Church possesses the right to make binding pronouncements on economic and social questions. And if indeed it has the right, we must determine exactly what this implies. This first chapter is concerned to examine these important questions.

The Church and social policy

The question is asked again and again: has the Church really an authority of its own in economic and social questions? What right has it to mix in matters that are really none of its concern? The Church should keep itself to its pastoral duties: proclaim the gospel, celebrate religious services, administer the sacraments and look after families and people in their individual needs and sorrows. The Church defends itself energetically if politics get involved in ecclesiastical matters. But then should not the Church stay clear of politics? The suspicion is often expressed that involvement in economic and social questions shows the Church's latent desire for power. It is claimed that the Church has surrendered its religious and moral authority in our society and is seeking to recover lost ground by exercising political and social influence.

On the other hand, many people complain that the Church's official representatives, the Pope and the bishops, say nothing about important political and social questions or join in the general discussion too late or do not articulate the Church's stand with sufficient decisiveness. The examples have been put forward of the debate about disarmament and the question of mass unemployment.

There are those who go a step further and demand of the Church direct support for certain social groups and immediate – including financial – aid for so-called freedom movements. They argue that the Church would be following Christ's example and, like him it ought to take the part of the poor, the oppressed and those who are despised by society. The Church could not and should not remain politically neutral, indeed, it should be 'partisan' in the sense of intervening on behalf of the poor and oppressed, as has been exemplarily shown in the Latin American Church in the great conferences of Medellin and Puebla.

Jesus no social revolutionary

Considering the way that Jesus spoke up for the poor and social fringe groups, the question arises whether this way of taking sides should also be seen in a sense as an attempt to exercise political influence. That would take no account of the fact that Jesus refused time and again to be taken up by the political and revolutionary goals of the zealots and other political groups. Although Jesus understood the Messianic expectations of Israel to refer expressly to himself, he still rejected out of hand any connection of himself with any political interpretation of the Messiah and his reign. We can, and indeed we must, consider the account of the temptations as related in the synoptic gospels (Matthew, Mark and Luke), immediately after his baptism in the Jordan and just before the beginning of his ministry, also as an early Christian analysis of Jesus' message and its political interpretation and relevance. Jesus refuses to turn the stones into bread or to seek social influence or political power. This could remove any New Testament basis for either a social revolutionary or an immediately socio-political understanding of the person and work of Jesus. Throughout his ministry Jesus rejected uncompromisingly every attempt to involve him politically, regardless of the direction, and refused to resort to political means. The final consequence of this course of action was Jesus' death on the cross. And yet the preacher Jesus is not apolitical. Jesus may not have been a social revolutionary, but his message and the proclaimed and living kingdom of God is of political consequence.

To put it another way: where the gospel is proclaimed and practised, it has social, communal, political and naturally also economic implications. The message of Jesus is dedicated to a comprehensive change of all human and social relationships. At the very beginning of the gospel message there is the call to conversion: 'The time is fulfilled, and the kingdom of God is at hand; repent, and believe in the gospel' (Mark 1: 15). The precondition of the kingdom of God is conversion, which means the complete renewal of all human relationships. There can be no doubt that this conversion must also have very solid effects on social and political life, for the kingdom of God is not something that exists in a space severed from solid social bearings; no, *the kingdom of God is in the midst of us*, in the middle of our social and political reality.

Prophetic pronouncements, the criticism of society and the desire to shape social organization have been part of the message of the kingdom of Israel and the reign of the Messiah since the time that Israel was chosen. Prophetic preaching in the Old Testament is concerned directly with the nation's social and political relationships. It is social criticism that finds legitimacy and orientation in the election of Israel as much as in the compulsion of divine law. This social criticism in the New Testament is, when compared with the attitudes of Old Testament prophets, conceived rather more individualistically, but still there is no doubt that Jesus' proclamation of the one kingdom of God also calls for changes in social relationships. It is true that the social responsibility of the Christian is not brought to the fore in the New Testament; nevertheless, the New Testament writings leave no doubt as to their clarity regarding the effects of faith on actual Christian life. The kingdom of God proclaimed by Jesus points towards a total change in individual conduct and in relationships within the community.

Prophetic office to ensure well-being

Even though there may be particular open questions concerning the Church's competence in economic and social matters, it is not reasonable to question whether the Church has a general social and economic responsibility at all. We have, however, to consider how far this public charge goes and how it can be defended theologically and exercised in an objectively competent way. Clear guidelines were laid down by Pius XI in his social encyclical of 1931 *Quadragesimo Anno* (No. 41-42). First of all, the Pope confirms the teaching laid down by Leo XIII in his encyclical *Rerum Novarum* which says: 'By law and by duty we exercise the power of our supreme authority of jurisdiction over social and economic questions.' The Pope then goes on to say that, as much on the grounds of revealed truth as of the divine mission to proclaim the moral code in full, the social and economic fields are also subject to the Church's 'very highest legal judgment'. To put it another way: economic and social questions, too, are subject to the Church's infallible teaching.

However, the Pope makes it very clear that Church authority in these matters is not unlimited. It does not refer to purely 'earthly matters' and 'questions of a technical nature' but to practical concerns based on the moral code and revealed truth. The encyclical recognizes the so-called 'law unto itself' of culturally factual phenomena such as economics, politics, art and sport. The Second Vatican Council paid tribute in its pastoral constitution to what it called 'the autonomy of earthly realities' and regretted earlier failures in Church attitudes (the Galileo affair). Art should therefore be judged according to aesthetic laws and the economy by the laws of economics.

From the relative independence of the economy and other fields of activity, the conclusion should not be drawn that they are therefore beyond moral judgement. There are *no* fields free of ethical values. As soon as human beings enter these fields as active figures, their deeds are subject to moral qualification. It should not be too difficult to realize that fact today, when even sport has become political. However, we have to judge quite clearly between the ethical and economic evaluation of how the economy is run. It is certainly not asserted in any way that the economy cannot therefore be subjected to ethical evaluation.

In practice it looks something like this. Let us take as an example the contemporary problem of mass unemployment. Where there is unemployment of millions of people willing to work, the socio-ethical situation is unacceptable. The right to work is a socio-ethical postulate; as a human right it is anchored in the personal dignity of each human being and it has been consistently defended by the Church, most recently in the encyclical upon work of *Laborum*

Exercens (No. 18). However, the realization of this ethical postulate is dependent on the real possibilities of the economy. Because of its prophetic role the Church can and must draw attention to the present situation and call to account those responsible, in particular management and unions, but also the politicians and social institutions. It cannot, however, prescribe a specific solution. For instance, it cannot take part in actual wage conflict on the grounds of its authority as a teacher, because it does not have this kind of economic or technical competence: its competence is ethical.

Where it has the resources the Church, because of its pastoral responsibilities, can certainly offer to help the afflicted and make suggestions for solutions, but it cannot make the decisions as to what are the best or the quickest ways of achieving the goal. If it comes to solving a really complex problem there are usually various possibilities. Here no-one has the right to claim, as *Gaudium et Spes*, No. 43, puts it, 'Church authority solely for himself and for his opinion'.

The Church's social teaching provides overall moral guidance. Its first duty is to proclaim the fundamental principles of community life and to protest against any violation regardless of the importance of who is involved. It lays down guidelines for the constitution of the social order and places out of bounds negative solutions and ideas inconsistent with a Christian and humane view of the human race. It has no specific authority for determining the details of how particular social orders should be worked out in practice. The Church's preaching on social matters thus should not be taken as an uncalled-for and impractical meddling in economic or political questions, or indeed as a demonstration of the Church's power, but as an expression of the maintenance of its responsibility for humanity, as its socially-critical prophetic office exercised in the interests and well-being of all.

What the Church says

Pius XI: encyclical *Quadragesimo Anno*

'Indeed, "the Church holds that it is unlawful for her to mix without cause in the temporal concerns"; however, she can in no wise renounce the duty God entrusted to her to interpose her authority, not of course in matters of technique for which she is neither suitably equipped nor endowed by office, but in all things that are connected with the moral law. For as to these, the deposit of truth that God committed to Us and the grave duty of disseminating and interpreting the whole moral law, and of urging it in season and out of season, bring under and subject to Our supreme jurisdiction not only social order but economic activities themselves.

'Even though economics and moral science employ each its own principles in its own sphere, it is, nevertheless, an error to say that the economic and social orders are so distinct from and alien to each other that the former depends in no way on the latter. Certainly the laws of economics, as they are termed, being based on the very nature of material things and on the capacities of the human body and mind, determine the limits of what productive human effort cannot, and of what it can attain in the economic field and by what means. Yet it is reason itself that clearly shows, on the basis of the individual and social nature of things and of men, the purpose which God ordained for all economic life.'

On the autonomy of earthly realities, cf. Second Vatican Council, Pastoral Constitution *Gaudium et Spes*, No. 36.

2. What do the Holy Scriptures say about the economic and social order?

'We must obey God rather than men'

The scriptures and the natural law are the 'sources' of Catholic social teaching, from which it derives its socio-ethical declarations and norms. For a long time it argued almost entirely on the basis of natural law, i.e., on the basis of common sense and the Christian philosophy concerning society. The social encyclicals up to and including Pacem in Terris *(1963) are eloquent witness to this. Now the Second Vatican Council has, within the framework of theology overall, led to a reconsideration of the scriptures. From this there arises for the social teaching of the Church a highly complex question: do the scriptures contain rules for communal and economic life? And how can these be applied to relations in industrial society?*

The words of the Apostle Peter before the Sanhedrin 'We must obey God rather than men' (Acts 5:29) have a timeless significance. They are a declaration with a programme which should be seen, against the New Testament background, as an ultimately unbridgeable tension between God's kingdom and the laws of this world. The disciples of Jesus live by the new law that Jesus has proclaimed. Their lives in this world are oriented to the message of God's kingdom. Is that relevant also for economic, social and political life, or has that kingdom of God only transitory power of compulsion for private, religious and family affairs? There can be no doubt that the gospel should, like yeast, ferment everything, and that goes for the state and the economy as well. It is for that reason that we face the question of the New Testament's socio-ethical instructions. Do the scriptures also lay down hard and fast rules for the Christian's economic and political relations, or do they just have general admonitions about loving one's neighbour and brotherliness? In a word: do the scriptures teach only about charity or also about social ethics? This fundamental and comprehensive question attains a particular aptness because of liberation theology in Latin America, which seeks to base its legitimacy and the setting of its socio-political goals immediately on the scriptures.

The appeal to scripture

As we all know, the scriptures contain no detailed teaching about economics or politics as such. Revelation should not be seen in the first place as a specific system of ideas – or to put it another way, an ideology. It consists in the proclamation that the promised kingdom of God was brought into the world by Jesus of Nazareth. The absence of concrete directions concerning economics and politics has led in the past to the teaching of the Church being argued almost exclusively from a socio-philosophical standpoint, closer to natural law, and less biblically or theologically. Apart from a few attempts, in the Catholic field there was really no social 'theology' in the true sense of the word. On the other hand, Catholic social philosophy could not be unbiblical, because it was and remains tied to revelation by means of the Christian view of humanity.

The Second Vatican Council has taken up the relevance of the biblical movement and set in motion a comprehensive rethinking of theology on a scriptural basis. The Council reminds us that scripture should be the starting point, medium and goal of the Christian message and moral teaching. For instance, in the rules or priestly training, it is required that individual theological disciplines 'be based anew on a more live contact with the mystery of Christ and the message of salvation' (No. 16). This call for a new biblical orientation has also been fully taken up by the Church's social teaching. The most recent proclamations on this teaching, for instance the encyclical of John Paul II about human work, *Laborem Exercens*, have been thoroughly worked out biblically and theologically. That does, however, give rise to the question: do the scriptures really give direct instructions on social and economic life which can be turned into concrete economic and social policy? How can we transfer to our modern relationships the assertions of scripture which are tied to their time? And then the still more difficult question: what is to be done about difficult issues, such as industrial co-responsibility on which the scriptures are silent?

The scriptures are no social catechism

Every attempt to use the scriptures as a social catechism in which one can find a detailed answer for every social and economic question is doomed to failure. In the first place scripture always makes pronouncements linked to the day to day problems of the communities of the particular time and historical situation of the people of Israel. To discover the guidance for all time revealed in scripture, we must go to the roots of its pronouncements and understand the principles that led to their being made. One cannot simply put its isolated rulings into a composite picture like some sort of puzzle or mosaic – a fond pastime in years gone by. Above all, it is quite wrong to give a fundamentalist interpretation to the scriptures, seeking to apply word for word and literally those directives, concrete and binding for their time, on the communal and economic issues of today.

Ventures of this kind have been characteristic of radical and utopian movements at all times and have invariably led to violence and dogmatic intolerance, as in the case of Thomas Müntzer and the Anabaptists, or else they have come to a halt in the face of reality. In this connection it is interesting to note the attempt by the respected Protestant theologian Karl Barth, who has directly related the 'civic communities and Christian communities' and has made the pronouncements of revelation analogously applicable to social realities (process of analogy — *analogia fidei*). This has not been satisfactory, because it was not secure against arbitrary and optional interpretation of the analogical possibilities. In this way, Karl Barth deduced from the variety of the gifts of the Holy Spirit the democratic division of power and from the revelatory nature of faith the ban on secret diplomacy.

All such attempts have failed. The scriptures cannot be applied as a comprehensive and exact social pattern and economic policy for the tremendously complicated and variegated procedures of the modern world. That is why the Church's social teaching by its very

43

nature asks the help of the secular social sciences and Christian social philosophy (natural law).

The Sermon on the Mount

There is a particular problem, so far as the Christian social message is concerned, in the radical demands of the Sermon on the Mount. On the one hand, it is not admissible to deradicalize them and to remove their critical sharpness by saying they are applicable only to some people (monks and nuns for instance) or that they apply only to private life and not to politics. Luther, for example, in his doctrine of the two kingdoms, chose the latter course. He said: As a Christian I have to live by the Sermon on the Mount in all its radicality, but as a member of society in the public arena that is not possible and would lead to chaos, because then the state would have to let evil-doers run free. That is why Luther, as is well known, prescribed natural law – which he strongly rejected elsewhere – as the compulsory standard in the public domain for Christians as well. But the way that Luther chose is not entirely satisfactory because it leads to an unacceptable double morality.

Christians are subject to the precepts of the Sermon on the Mount in both private and political life and have to ask themselves how to give reality to its message in their daily existence. A literal interpretation is not possible and cannot be intended, for the Sermon on the Mount not only lays down the renunciation of revenge and the duty of unconditional love for one's enemies, but also: 'If your right eye causes you to sin, pluck it out and throw it away' (Matt. 5:29). There are other examples that could be mentioned. Hence we have to grasp more accurately what socio-ethical instructions are being given for our life in the world and try, as far as possible, to bring Jesus' message into practical politics.

Socio-ethical instructions

It follows from what has been said so far that the scriptures do not contain an actual 'juridical code' but the 'principles of law' (Erik Wolf) for economic and social life, i.e., fundamental thoughts and guidelines for regulating our social lives. It is our task to take the directives of scripture, linked to their own time and situation, and turn them into socio-ethical precepts and general directives that go beyond time, and then see how they are applicable to economic and social policy today. In doing so we shall not be able to do without the aid of the secular social sciences and Christian social philosophy (natural law).

We can welcome current interest in a louder proclamation of the scriptures' social significance and the real message of Jesus, but we should not forget that scriptural directives are not so unequivocal that they cannot lead to contradictory interpretations. The interpretation and realization of natural law, too often thoughtlessly rejected, has experienced the same difficulties. We must not forget that the same mistakes made in the name of natural law have also been made in the name of scripture. We need only think of how the problem of slavery was dealt with. On the basis of past experience we can doubt whether, simply taken on its own, scripture is capable of helping us out of our present difficulties without our falling into serious errors. The Marxist Sandinista policy of Nicaragua gives us an example, having support from Ernesto and Fernando Cardinal expressly in the name of the gospel. Political theology of this kind always ends nowhere and not infrequently leads to the legitimation of a policy directly in opposition to the gospel spirit.

What the Church says

Second Vatican Council, Dogmatic Constitution *Dei Verbum*

'Sacred theology relies on the written Word of God, taken together with sacred tradition, as on a permanent foundation. By this Word it is most firmly strengthened and constantly rejuvenated, as it searches out, under the light of faith, the full truth stored up in the mystery of Christ ... The ministry of the Word, too – pastoral preaching, catechetics and all forms of Christian instruction, among which the liturgical homily should hold pride of place – is healthily nourished and thrives in holiness through the Word of Scripture' (No. 24).

John Paul II, encyclical *Redemptor Hominis*

'The Church, which lives from an eschatological faith, considers man's concern for its humanity, for the future of humanity on earth, and together with that also the direction of development and progress, as a vital element in its mission from which it may not be parted. The source of this concern the Church finds in Jesus Christ himself, as the Gospels witness. For this very reason the Church would like to strengthen this concern through its unity with Him as it interprets man's situation in the contemporary world according to the most important signs of our time' (No. 15).

Pius XII, Easter message on 1 June 1941

'It is part of the Church's unassailable area of jurisdiction to look into those interests of the social life that touch on the field of morality or are indeed concerned with it, and to judge whether the foundations of the existing social order are in accordance with the eternally valid order which God, the Creator and Redeemer, has brought into being by natural law and revelation. Both these are called on by Leo XIII in his letter (Rerum Novarum). And with right: for these foundations of the natural law and revealed truth, as two streams of water that are in no way opposed to each other but flow in the same direction, both have their common source in God' (Utz-Groner, No. 498).

3. John Paul II and the Christian view of humanity
'The truth we owe to humanity'

This chapter gives information on two important issues: the signifi-cance of the Christian view of humanity for Catholic social teaching and the method of procedure for such teaching. How does Catholic social teaching arrive at its socio-ethical standards and at its concrete guidelines for individual cases when the scriptures lay down no precise rules for our present industrial society? The Christian view of humanity is of central importance in this. It is the foundation of Catholic social teaching.

In his opening speech at the third general assembly of the Latin American bishops in Puebla, Mexico, on 28 January 1979, Pope John Paul II put down important and indispensible markers for Catholic social teaching. Against the background of Latin American relations and with a view to liberation theology, the Pope's utterances are of basic importance.

The Christian view of humanity

The Pope said that the truth we owe to humanity is in the first instance the revealed truth about humanity itself, i.e., the Christian view of men and women. The basis of this view is the teaching of 'man in the image of God, who as such cannot be reduced to a little piece of nature or an anonymous number in human society'. And man being made in the likeness of God differentiates Christian anthropology unmistakably from every other teaching, ideology or world view. This complete truth about humanity, i.e., the Christian view of men and women revealed to us, is the basis of social teaching and is, as the Pope said, the basis for the true liberation of the human race.

The Church's task is to defend and promote the inalienable dignity of human beings as God's image. The human being must be the centre of the economy, society and politics. As people are, according to Christian belief, not creatures subject to economic and social processing (as indeed they are according to the principles of materialism, Marxism and liberal capitalism); these phenomena must be arranged to accommodate human beings and be subject to their needs. The Pope extends these thoughts, only briefly alluded to here, in his encyclical *Laborem Exercens*, in which he urges that men and women, as workers, should not be subjugated to objective and material conditions and that labour is entitled to precedence over capital.

Ideological systems rejected

The Pope has laid down the Christian view of humanity as the basis of Catholic social teaching. Hence he unequivocally rejects all opposing opinions, whether they come from Latin America, Europe or anywhere else, which seek to interpret the Church's social teaching with the help of modern worldly systems or analyses of society alien to it. Individual whim may not select an ideological system or strategy for realizing the gospel's social message. Quite simply, the Church owes people the duty to proclaim the gospel's unchanging truth, which is not to be boiled down to a worldly philosophical system or a purely politico-social activity.

The Pope says that when the Church promotes human rights, development and social justice, it does so within the framework of its religious mission and not on the basis of some political commission. It therefore does not need to take refuge in ideological systems, because the gauge of its social activity has been revealed to it. To remain true to its religious mission the Church must remain free of ideological systems.

'Whatever may be the suffering and wretchedness that afflict humanity, Christ stands on the side of the poor, not with violence, intrigues or political systems, but with the truth about man, his road to a better future.'

Compassion for humanity and its total liberation also belong to the Church's mission, but one must not limit the gospel message of liberation to the economic, political, social or cultural dimension. So that the original message of Christian liberation is not trimmed or watered down, the Pope urges that every kind of (ideological) trimming and (political) equivocation be avoided, otherwise the Church would lose its fundamental significance and the Christian liberation message would have no more originality, so that it could easily be taken over and manipulated by ideological systems (cf. *Evangelii Nuntiandi*, No. 33).

Standards for social life

The Pope further explains in his speech that Church social teaching comes from 'the light of God's Word and the authentic magisterium, from the presence of Christians in the midst of the world's changing situations and their immediate involvement with the tasks arising from it', and that it contains 'principles for reflection and also standards for the development of proper judgment and guidelines for effective initiatives.'

He refers to Catholic social teaching as a science of standards; the standards and guidelines for social and economic life are laid down and from these it develops strategies for constantly improving social justice in every walk of life and for everyone. Where do these standards come from? Two sources: the teachings of the scriptures and recognition of Christian natural law. Together they form the determining ingredients and the basis of social teaching.

In dealing with actual problems it is rare that the scriptures themselves give us specific guidance in a direct manner. In such cases the social proclamation has to refer to the Christian view of humanity, the basis of social teaching. Often it will be quite enough to go back to key ideas of Catholic social teaching, such as the principles of the value of the person, solidarity, subsidiarity and the common good, to determine where the solution may be found. For these social principles are basically nothing more than the summary of the Christian view of humanity which is at the centre of Catholic social teaching.

In the light of the gospel

It is often assumed that Catholic social teaching is an all-enveloping system rather like a textbook on economics or political science. This is not so. It is far more a set of principles. It aims at putting forward in correct order the foundations for a political and social order in accord with social justice and human dignity. Its methodology confirms this. In dealing with actual issues it takes account of actual social relations or looks – as the Council puts it – for the 'signs of the times'. This methodology, unlike the claim frequently made, is common to liberation theology. One always has to start with the analysis (using the social sciences) of existing social relationships. In the second stage, these analyses or social trends are tested and evaluated, as the Council says, 'in the light of the gospel'. This means referring back to the critical yardstick of the Christian view of humanity and its social principles as well as its other socio-ethical principles. In this way practical solutions can be reached for particular problems and, where necessary, a strategy can be worked out for social issues.

No baptism of Marxism

The Christian view of humanity is unalterable, *sui generis*, and not to be replaced by philosophical systems. This must be borne in mind in every kind of social, political and economic activity, for behind every issue there stands a certain view of humanity which determines its structure, goal and strategy. It is therefore in principle impossible to interpret the goal of Christian community reform with replacement pieces of Marxist ideology. It is even less thinkable to baptize Marxism after the event, as has been attempted by some. The Christian and Marxist view of humanity are incompatible, hence one has to avoid an incautious involvement with Marxism. It has its own orientation and ideology based on a very different view of humanity.

We should be grateful to the Pope for his clear words. If the Church were to believe that in the present situation, or in certain regional issues, it will reach people better if it toys with experiments of this nature, it will put at risk the originality of its message and in the end lose everything.

Worldly philosophies of salvation are many: we do not need to use the Church to invent a new one.

What the Church says

John Paul II, Address to the Third General Assembly of Latin American Bishops, Puebla, 28 January 1979:

'Thanks to the Gospel of joy, the Church possesses the truth about human beings. It finds it in its own anthropology, which the Church never tires of deepening and proclaiming. The basic teaching of this anthropology is the doctrine that the human being is the image of God, which as such cannot be reduced to a small part of nature or an anonymous cypher of the human community . . . The full truth of mankind constitutes the foundation of the Church's social teaching; at the same time it is the basis of a true liberation. In the light of this truth the human being is not a creation subject to economic and political processes, but these processes are shaped for human beings and subordinate to them' (I,9).

'On the other hand we bear in mind that the Church's intervention in areas such as the promotion of being human, the development, justice and right of the person, is always intended to serve human beings, the human beings who it makes its own, as the Church sees them in the Christian concept of anthropology. The Church therefore does not need to take refuge in systems and ideologies to love, defend, and help give reality to, the liberation of human beings' (III, 2).

Paul VI, Apostolic Letter *Evangelii Nuntiandi*

'With regard to the liberation which evangelization proclaims and strives to put into practice one should rather say this: it cannot be contained in the simple and restricted dimension of economics, politics, social or cultural life; it must envisage the whole man, in all his aspects, right up to and including his openness to the absolute, even the divine Absolute; it is therefore attached to a certain concept of man, to a view of man which it can never sacrifice to the need of any strategy, practice or short-term efficiency' (No. 33).

4. The theology of liberation and Catholic social teaching

Is the theology of liberation which originated in Latin America, and is now spread worldwide, compatible with Catholic social teaching or even part of it? Or should it be rejected for fundamental reasons? These questions will be answered in what follows. This article, published before the appearance of the two instructions of the Congregation of the Faith on the theology of liberation (6 August 1984 and 22 March 1986), places this theology within the context of Catholic social teaching.

Medellin and Puebla

What *is* liberation theology? Such a precise question cannot be answered clearly because this theology does not exist as a unitary idea. There are in fact a number of individual theologians and different outlines of thought, but no clearly definable 'theology of liberation'. It is just as hard to answer clearly whether it is compatible with Catholic social teaching or whether one can even regard it as a legitimate branch. It is therefore an error to speak of *the* 'theology of liberation' in the singular and to either praise it without stint or damn it unequivocally.

It is in its way a new structure in theological thinking and Christian action which had its origin in Latin America and is bound up historically with the theological and social uprising of the Church in Latin America at the bishops' conference in Medellin, Colombia, in 1968. Although the Medellin documents avoid the concept of liberation theology, it was at this conference that the codeword *liberación* (liberation) became the key concept.

A certain amount of clarification and an interim solution of the, until then, stormy theological and socio-political debate followed the bishops' conference in Puebla, Mexico, in 1979, which placed the overall theme under the general concept of 'evangelization'.

Practical theology

Liberation theology could be called a practical theology. As such it is nothing new, though it is a new way of thinking theologically and relating to Christian practice. It regards itself as a grass roots theology, something growing out of practice, and it wants to be understood as a 'critical reflection on "practice" '. It is not founded on theological learning or dogma, but practice and precisely the practice of liberation. It is a critical-theological reflection of the Christian community, which has seen the struggle for human liberation in Latin America as a Christian imperative and, later, reflects upon and gives a theological basis to its involvement.

It does not start, then, from theology to throw light on social practice but the other way round. The dependence and oppression of the people and indeed the fight for their total freedom are theologically interpreted, and in particular with reference to God's redeeming and liberating action. The social sciences take over the traditional role of philosophy. At the heart lies the analysis of socio-economic relationships, usually on the basis of Marxist social criticism. It is claimed that it is not enough in Latin America to alter people individually, because first of all we have to alter the social, economic and political structures, so that people have the opportunity to change themselves. Liberation from want and oppression is the preliminary to their religious and theological liberation.

Liberación

The Latin American liberation campaign is seen from the point of view of the chosen people in the Old and New Testaments. The starting point of most theological considerations is the Exodus of the people of Israel from Egypt, the liberation from bondage, suppression and captivity. Israel experiences its liberation as Yahweh's act of deliverance. Yahweh makes Israel the chosen people and in so doing creates its political existence; the political aspect is included in the religious act of achieving nationhood and political liberation includes the religious aspect.

Against this background, Christ's act of redemption is comprehensively interpreted as religious, social and political liberation,

elucidating and giving substance in its social and political consequences to the Christian freedom (*libertas christiana*) of which
the Apostle Paul speaks. The prophets' socially critical message
and Jesus' plea on behalf of the poor and despised compel the
Christian to unremitting criticism of social injustice and persecution
and to unconditional solidarity with the needy and oppressed.

The liberation from captivity promised for the time of the Messiah
(Isa. 42:2-7) and the eschatological event of the new creation of
heaven and earth imply, on the one hand, criticism of existing
social relationships and, on the other, that the human race, social
relationships and the structures of the community have become
new. Through Christ's act of salvation the kingdom of God is now
with us, and it follows that the Church's mission is not only to
proclaim that kingdom but also to ensure that God rules here and
now in communal and economic structures.

God in the revolution?

In this we touch on a sensitive nerve of liberation theology. It is
quite legitimate to relate the history of salvation to that of the world,
and redemption in Christ to liberation from political oppression
and social injustice.

But if we identify one with the other, emancipatory and revolutionary liberation becomes a vehicle for Christ's liberating redemption and the technical and social progress of civilization
proclaims itself as the evolution of God's kingdom. In a manner
of speaking, the redeeming God meets the Christian in the political-
revolutionary fight for liberation (Gustavo Gutierrez). This creates
the danger that the transcendental quality of redemption in Christ
is dissolved in the immanence of emancipatory and revolutionary
social liberation. The distinction is not to be seen in quantitative
temporal terms but qualitative eschatological terms. The kingdom
of God can never, in any circumstances, be the outcome of an
evolutionary process of technology and civilization. Furthermore,
the idea of God being in the revolutionary process is untenable if
we are to take seriously the message of the Sermon on the Mount,
the gospel of non-violence.

A new social teaching?

After what has been said, the question of the reconcilability of liberation theology with Church social teaching cannot be answered with a plain yes or no. Catholic social teaching has always seen its task as liberating people from humiliating and degrading social, economic and communal relationships. The campaign for the rights of workers in Europe during the 19th century was fought with other concepts and arguments, but the goal was and remains the same.

The method, too, is not as different as it appears at first glance, because it always started with an economic and social analysis. From that flowed a call for solutions that would be in line with the Christian message. Catholic social teaching sees its task as being responsible for the faith in the context of the social world, taking up advocacy for the poor and the socially oppressed, and so fulfilling its prophetic office of protector against social injustice and injury to human rights.

From this viewpoint, liberation theology is the legitimate off-spring of Catholic social teaching. It could be described as a preliminary Christian social doctrine, a guide to a specific interpretation of social teaching for Latin America, but no more than a guide, because only basic conditions for general human liberation have so far been reflected upon theologically. At most all that has been achieved is partial suggestions for the concrete renewal of society and the economy, and these have been more or less inspired by Marxism.

And this is where at the same time the necessary reservations begin. True, the number of real Marxists is not very great, but the lure of Marxist-Socialist oriented experiments is nonetheless generally very strong. As the Nicaraguan example shows, making deals with Marxist-communist groups is not possible; Christians always draw the short straw if they really adhere to the gospel.

There is the further danger that the message of Jesus is reduced to an ideological programme. Turning the political and the social into absolutes contravenes the spirit of the New Testament, which indeed incorporates the message of freedom, but Christian salvation is in a totally different category from liberation seen purely as social emancipation. And to attempt to interpret the gospel in a Marxist way would be tantamount to trying to cast out devils in the name of Beelzebub.

What the Church says

Congregation for the Doctrine of the Faith, Instruction on Certain Aspects of the Theology of Liberation, *Libertatis Nuntius*

'The Gospel of Jesus Christ is a message of freedom and a force for liberation. In recent years, this essential truth has become the object of reflection for theologians, with a new kind of attention which is itself full of promise.

'Liberation is first and foremost liberation from the radical slavery of sin. Its end and its goal is the freedom of the children of God, which is the gift of grace. As a logical consequence, it calls for freedom from many different kinds of slavery in the cultural, economic, social and political spheres, all of which derive ultimately from sin, and so often prevent people from living in a manner befitting their dignity' (Introduction).

Congregation for the Doctrine of the Faith, *Instruction on Christian Freedom and Liberation (22 March 1986)*

'In the Old Testament, the liberating action of Yahweh which serves as model and reference for all others is the Exodus from Egypt, "the house of bondage". When God rescues his People from hard economic, political and cultural slavery, he does so in order to make them, through the Covenant on Sinai, "a kingdom of priests and a holy nation"' (Ex. 19:6).

'The major and fundamental event of the Exodus therefore has a meaning which is both religious and political. God sets his People free and gives them descendants, a land and a law, but within a Covenant and for a Covenant. One cannot therefore isolate the political aspect for its own sake; it has to be considered in the light of a plan of a religious nature within which it is integrated' (No. 44).

5. The Gospel – a political message?
The pros and cons of political theology

Quite apart from liberation theology, there is a 'political theology' which has sought public attention and which many see as a counterpart to Catholic social teaching and regard as a vehicle for change in social structure and for institutional criticism inside the Church. What is the characteristic starting point for 'political theology'? How can it be judged from the viewpoint of Catholic social teaching?

Political theology and Catholic social teaching, in the opinion of the Münster theologian Prof J. B. Metz, have the same concerns but quite different starting points. Both consider the responsibility of the faith with regard to contemporary social and communal structures, but while modern Catholic social teaching arose as a response to 19th century social problems, political theology wants to promote awareness of the social and political relevance of Christ's message. Do these two approaches have more in common than social and political concerns?

De-privatization of faith

Political theology feels itself committed to the emancipatory inheritance of the Enlightenment and has therefore allowed itself to be led by the 'critical theology' of the Frankfurt School and its neo-Marxist social criticism. It maintains that the relationship between faith and religion has been broken in the mind of contemporary public opinion, determined as it is by the Enlightenment and the philosophy of a dialectical interpretation of history (Marxism). The Church is claimed to have reacted to the Enlightenment passively and negatively, by being apologetic and one-sided over problems said to have been uncovered by the Enlightenment and to have withdrawn into itself, capitulating in front of challenges posed by new social conditions.

As the gospel is aimed at the public, however, it is worth resuming this dialogue with the Enlightenment and opening a serious debate with the dialectical philosophers and 19th century revolutionary-historical currents of opinion. The individualization of redemption (through the unilateral save-your-souls pastoral message) has been done to death in the past. For this reason Metz sees faith de-privatization as 'the first theologically critical task of political theology'. In fact, he wants this to be understood as applicable for every theology and theological discipline when it comes to assessing and realizing the social relevance of all aspects of the message of the faith. It follows that a purely individual theological or existential philosophical interpretation of the gospel message (as put forward by Bultmann) or a metaphysical interpretation (as put forward by Rahner) would not do justice to its fundamental social relevance.

As far as the thesis of de-privatization and the public nature of the gospel message goes, the concerns of political theology can be fully and heartily supported by Catholic social teaching, which is in itself the visible expression of the Church's wish to address the public at large and its social message (such as proclaimed for example in the social encyclicals) expressing in a clear and understandable way for everyone the relevance of the gospel.

The eschatological dimension

Political theology wants to bring to the fore the eschatological and futuristic nature of the New Testament message for the socially critical function of the faith. Salvation is something wonderful in the future, a radical-eschatological event that transforms all relationships, bringing about 'a new heaven and a new earth'. This implies relentless questioning of all the social structures, judicial systems and social relationships ever brought into being. From such an eschatological perspective, this (political) theology sets itself the task of releasing all liberating powers inherent in the gospel and achieving here and now the content of the Christian message of freedom. At the same time it would seek out, criticize and call to account all false claims to overlordship and dependency.

The doubtfulness and shortcomings of every social order must be brought under scrutiny so that the way can be made clear for an ever-better realization of social justice.

This interpretation wants Catholic social teaching to play an eminently important role. So far, so good! However, we find it unacceptable if Metz sees this as the only possible application of its role. Such a negative, purely critical, approach may be of value, yet social teaching cannot be satisfied with this, because it must also take the risk of giving a positive outline for a social order – something Metz emphatically rejects. It would not be in accordance with the Church's duty to proclaim the gospel if it were merely to play the role of a socially critical watchdog – and in the long run society would not accept that.

The Church as an institution for social criticism

On the platform of political theology, the Church is defined primarily as an institution of social criticism. True, it has exercised this criticism at all times, but never to the exclusion of everything else. Consequently, it is a matter for surprise that the Church should here be spoken of so positively as an institution.

What Metz intends to say, however, is that only an institution could exercise this function. It is not a matter of expressing society's needs and desires, but to speak out uncompromisingly about critical contradictions. In Metz's view there is a lack of critical-revolutionary potential in the Church. He feels that in the past it has taken up a position that is by and large 'counter-revolutionary, full of resentments and surly' towards society and the world. All too often it has, or so he claims, either failed to speak out critically or much too late if at all, exposing itself to the danger of being seen as an ideological superstructure over existing social relationships and power systems.

Critical questions

It is to be welcomed that, from the viewpoint of Christian social teaching, political theology has brought back so firmly into the Church's awareness, its public role, the social relevance of the gospel and the social responsibility of the faith. To that extent, it is useful as a part of fundamental theological preparation for social teaching. At other points, too, it can be fruitful, for instance when considering the socially-critical implications of the New Testament's eschatology: the promised new creation at the end of time constitutes a permanent questioning of all existing social institutions and structures.

One must be careful, however, about making the gospel message merely political. It is unclear, from the point of view of political theology, how such a politicization can be effectively prevented. Anyone proclaiming so vehemently the political nature of the gospel is utterly frivolous if they do not indicate how such developments can be made to stop short of a politicization of the Church. Indeed, there is quite sufficient warning in the Church's very negative experiences in the past in this field. The danger exists that criticism of the Church's being too conservative may all too easily become identification with a Church only intent on revolutionary emancipation.

It must also be asked if it is wise for the Church to be defined so pointedly as a court of social criticism. To be sure it is that, too, but this element does not stand on its own nor does it sufficiently describe the identity of the Church, which is first and foremost the community of the disciples of Jesus who through baptism and the eucharist are incorporated into the Body of Christ. To believe does not mean in the first instance social criticism, it means life with Christ in the community of the Church. Faith calls for identification with Christ, his gospel and the fellowship of the Church.

As experiences in recent times have shown, any socially critical function which is isolated from the total application of the gospel message will develop, before you know where you are, into a religious organization well distanced from the Church. For many young people political theology (misunderstood) has become a comfortable alibi: 'Jesus, yes! Church, no!'

Many people, and not all of them young either, regard political theology in the meanwhile as the programme of a counter-church. If a specific social revolutionary and left-wing political message is then combined with precepts of social criticism, the programme for turning the Christian message into an ideology is complete. A good deal of self-criticism would not be out of place here.

What the Church says

Second Vatican Council, *Pastoral Constitution Gaudium et Spes*

'Therefore, while we are warned that it profits a man nothing if he gain the whole world and lose himself, the expectation of a new earth must not weaken but rather stimulate our concern for cultivating this one. For here grows the body of a new human family, a body which even now is able to give some foreshadowing of the new age. Earthly progress must be carefully distinguished from the growth of Christ's kingdom. Nevertheless, to the extent that the former can contribute to the better ordering of human society, it is of vital concern to the kingdom of God' (No. 39).

International Theological Commission, *Relations between Human Development and Christian Salvation (1977)*

'The Church ... is not bound exclusively and inseparably to any race or nation, to any particular way of life, to any customary pattern of living either old or new. In virtue of its origin, supernatural character, religious mission and eschatological hope, it cannot be confounded with any socio-political system or linked with it by necessary, unbreakable ties. If the Church must be careful not to be entrapped by the power seekers, no more ought it to surrender to sheer neutrality or unsympathetic detachment and retire to a purely non-political role' (No. 45,c).

6. Subsidiarity as a vital principle of free social communities

Among the basic elements of Catholic social teaching are principles of human dignity, solidarity, the common good and subsidiarity. These social principles arise from the Christian view of humanity, but they could also be described as focal points for that view. The principle of subsidiarity occupies a very special position in the development and tradition of Catholic social teaching, and for this reason it is often described also as that teaching's classical social principle.

Freedom as a basic value

Political constitution is not an act of the unfettered imagination which takes place in a social space without predetermining factors. Any who venture into the field of putting society in order and start planning how to improve it, first have to have clear ideas about the various economic, social, demographic and cultural factors involved, if they are not to build castles in the air.

Among the most important values in the Western world is its enormous need for freedom. Every economic plan, every design for the community, be it ever so sensible and desirable, is doomed if it is not accepted freely. For a government to push something through may be tolerated, but imposition of a complete system curtailing freedom and not based on the capacity of the people to decide for themselves will fail to gain essential public support. Among the fundamental values of Western democratic communities, freedom is top priority.

This basic attitude generally agrees with the Christian view of humanity. Men and women are made to be free. According to the message of the Creation, humanity has the choice between good and evil; it can even decide against God. As people have the gift of freedom, they are responsible for what they do and do not do. God calls humanity to account: 'What is this that you have done?' (Gen. 3:13).

Freedom is a constituent part of being human, while animals are driven by instinct. Freedom is an inalienable human right and so a social order can be described as human and worthy of humankind, if it gives its citizens the maximum amount of room for personal self-development, economic and social decision-sharing and political co-responsibility.

Subsidiarity

The social principle of subsidiarity is one of the most important structural principles of free social communities that respect human dignity. Subsidiarity is in the fullest sense of the word a democratic principle. A really democratic society or state is unthinkable without a structure, organization and division of tasks based on subsidiarity. Subsidiarity is often described as the classical heart of Catholic social teaching. The word derives from the Latin 'subsidium' which means giving support and assistance. The state and the social community, and for that matter every lesser authority, should interfere in a 'subsidiary' way, i.e., give assistance to a lower level organization (such as the family) only if that organization cannot meet its obligations by itself.

The 1931 encyclical *Quadragesimo Anno* gives the classical definition of this principle and lays down that 'every social activity ought of its very nature to furnish help to the members of the social body and never destroy or absorb them' (No. 79).

Accordingly, it is not the duty of the state and public authority to draw all tasks to itself and control the life of the community dirigistically and centrally. The principle of subsidiarity demands rather that, as far as is possible, tasks should be delegated and private initiative be encouraged and supported. That applies to every social organization, including the Church, a point all too often gladly ignored. The principle of subsidiarity is a general social principle in a free society conscious of the dignity of humankind.

A society based on the principle of subsidiarity

Catholic social teaching aims at a pluralistic society with a multiplicity of social orders, associations and institutions both vertically and horizontally. The community and its governmental institutions should be structured in a manner which facilitates subsidiarity, i.e., they should be built from the bottom upwards in order to guarantee the maximum development of the individual and the individual's ability and to secure the existence of smaller communities, such as the family and private institutions.

A society based on the principle of subsidiarity must, therefore, ensure that higher authority and social organizations only take on tasks which cannot be satisfactorily carried out at a lower level.

Any effort from above to interfere unnecessarily with the affairs of those lower down the scale must be prevented. In particular, it is important to control the unlimited growth of state activity. In this way the state can carry out its proper tasks, those which it alone can do as the supreme social authority. An all-present welfare state is not a Christian ideal.

The subdivision of responsibilities between the state, the community and social organizations should be regulated strictly according to the principles of subsidiarity: priority should go to communities or institutions that are smaller or at a lower level, then those at the next stage up, and finally those at governmental level. The principle of subsidiarity, reasonably applied, also means that wherever lower level social groups or institutions are unable to fulfil their duties, they pass them on to others.

Mass society and democracy

Size seems to be the fate of modern industrial society. There is a worldwide trend towards enormous numbers of people living in overwhelming conurbations, indeed mega-cities. The urbanization of the world population is proceeding at an unforeseen pace, so that in developing countries such as Colombia and Mexico more than half the population lives in cities. Conurbations like Sao Paulo and Mexico City are likely to have at today's estimates populations of between 20 and 30 million by the year 2000.

Even if one is sceptical about the predictions of futurologists, novelists and science fiction films, it still seems likely that the mass society of tomorrow will be a graded, bureaucratized world vulnerable to manipulation if the trend is not decisively countered. There are already a number of outsize cities that have to all intents and purposes become ungovernable. Talk of the concrete jungle is not just idle chatter. A city like New York has become a nightmare for those who have to govern it. It is commonly asserted that crime in such big cities is no longer effectively fought but merely regimented, and mass misery is not being eradicated, just controlled.

One of the promising therapies for modern mass society is consistent application of the principle of subsidiarity, because it is an effective counterbalance to centralization, bureaucratization and over-development. It really is a matter of encouraging, strengthening or creating units that are small and capable of being controlled.

Consistent application of subsidiarity can strengthen democracy. It means delegation of authority and responsibility, and therefore the division and control of power. Subsidiarity is a highly democratic principle and, what is more, profoundly human. If modern mass society wants to respect human dignity, this principle must be taken extremely seriously.

What the Church says

Pius XI, encyclical *Quadragesimo Anno*

'As history abundantly proves, it is true that on account of changed conditions many things that were done by small associations in former times cannot be done now save by large associations. Still, that most weighty principle, which cannot be set aside or changed, remains fixed and unshaken in social philosophy: just as it is gravely wrong to take from individuals what they can accomplish by their own initiative and industry and give it to the community, so also is it an injustice and at the same time a grave evil and disturbance of right order to assign to a greater and higher association what lesser and subordinate organizations can do. For every social activity ought of its very nature to furnish help to the members of the social body, and never destroy or absorb them' (No. 79).

'The supreme authority of the State ought, therefore, to let subordinate groups handle matters and concerns of lesser importance, which would otherwise dissipate its effort greatly. Thereby the State will more freely, powerfully and effectively do all those things that belong to it alone because it alone can do them' (No. 80).

7. Human dignity and work (personality)

The human being as a person and as the image of God

This chapter deals with the principle of personality. The notion of the individual as a person and as the image of God lies at the very heart of Catholic social teaching. The personal worth of the human being is unassailable, an inescapable yardstick for every aspect of Christian social policy, making the principle of personality of permanent value to that teaching.

All the many differing and competing social concepts and socio-political goals are based on varying views of humanity. It is these views which, ultimately, form concrete social policies and the basic structures for established social orders. For Catholic social teaching humanity's transcendental origin, and the resulting reference to God in the Christian view of humanity, are of crucial importance.

Creation and the image of God

On the very first pages the scriptures report in the story of Creation: 'So God created man in his own image, in the image of God he created them; male and female he created them' (Gen. 1:27).

The human being is God's creation. That is the first and fundamental utterance of the scriptures about humanity. It utterly rejects every materialistic interpretation (Marxism, Darwinism) which seeks to look at humanity without any relation to God. The origin and goal of human life is neither humanity itself nor any power that exists beside or independent of God: it is God the Creator.

God created human beings in his own image. In that lies their incomparable value, as the image of God. Scripture does not wish to express anything more than that when it states that human beings shall 'have dominion' over the earth (Gen. 1:28). And this does not mean absolute and untrammelled power (the right to destroy the environment). Not at all! Scripture wants to say that between human beings and the rest of creation there is a qualitative difference: in worth and dignity, humanity transcends the whole of creation because it is made in the image of God and is, at the same time, his confidant, to whom God speaks as an equal.

The relation with God, humankind's transcendental openness, is an integral part of the Christian view and for that reason also an indispensable part of the social order. And so, for the Christian, the retort that 'religion is one's own affair' can never mean that the human being's religious relations are of only lesser or private significance and that therefore they have no role in the development of the social order. And it is in this that liberal and social education and social policy show time and again their cloven hoof. If transcendental openness lies at the very core of humanity, then religion is also a constituent element of life in the community, and any ban on religion from public life contradicts the essence of human nature.

God's co-workers

Human work is part of the value of humanity as the image of God. Looked at in the sense of the encyclical *Laborem Exercens*, this term is applicable to every aspect of human effort in and for the world. Humankind has been created by God to 'fill the earth and subdue it' (Gen. 1:28) and it has the specific cultural duty to 'till it and keep it' (Gen. 2:15). The scriptures see human beings as carrying God's mandate, and their labours are laid on them by God. The world is not presented as something that is just there ready for everyone. On the contrary, human beings have the duty to collaborate in the world's development. Because of that, they become in a certain sense God's co-workers (*Cooperator Dei*). And that gives human labour, and everyone who works, extraordinary value (cf. *Gaudium et Spes*, Nos. 34 and 67).

In his encyclical *Laborem Exercens* John Paul II added another thought: through work human beings become the image of God,

69

for 'Man is the image of God partly through the mandate received from his Creator to subdue, to dominate the earth. In carrying out this mandate, man, every human being, reflects the very action of the Creator of the universe' (No. 4). In this way work is ennobled, since it is a means for becoming God's image.

Thus this view of humanity and its work forms the basis of a high work ethic: the worker is the image of God and his co-worker in creation. Both Judaism and Christianity have never held the ancient world's view that manual labour is something dishonourable or demeaning. The apostles were all manual labourers of one kind or another; Jesus himself was the son of one and worked in the family workshop. Through him, work penetrates the mystery of the incarnation and redemption. This view means also that human beings have a great responsibility *vis-à-vis* the world of work. The Christian view of humanity urges us, further, to humanize working conditions. Anyone permitting working conditions that are unworthy of human beings is guilty of a sin against humanity as created in the image of God.

The principle of personality

The scriptures do not deal with philosophical ideas and categories, so that when they tell us that the human being has been created in the 'image of God' (*Imago Dei*), they mean exactly what we seek to express with the concept of personality. Human beings are God's image and partner. The incomparable value of humanity lies in the fact that God speaks to us and that we can reply. That is the foundation for human dignity, and it is also the basis of human personality, freedom and responsibility. For language, the ability to speak, is the crystallization of personality.

When we describe the human being as a person, we want thereby to say that it is intended for freedom and responsibility. Every single individual possesses an unassailable dignity which does not permit him or her, on any grounds whatever, to be subordinated to the demands of the economic process, socio-political goals, party doctrine or anything else of the kind. The principle of personality therefore rates as the very first principle of Catholic social teaching. In doing so it wants to affirm that for Christian social policy the personality of the individual is the indispensable guideline for the establishment of the economic and social order.

The rights of the worker

Workers' rights arise straight from the dignity of the person and of human labour. The Pope says that one must see them in connection with the rights that arise from human nature (*Laborem Exercens*, No. 16). Workers' rights belong, like social rights, to humanity's original rights and are, like them, inalienable and untouchable. Only some central aspects will be touched on here, as they cannot be treated in full at this point.

First of all, there is the right to work. It is a heavy duty for all those carrying responsibility in society and government to see to it that anyone who wants to work must be found a job. If it is right that the individual unfolds as a human person through work, so that such labour leads to the full development of the human being, then the loss of a job is at the same time a loss of human potential for development and participation in the community. This has been confirmed of late by research into the plight of the long-term unemployed. Social security money cannot make up for the social and cultural value of labour. Loss of a job means loss of dignity and self respect.

Another important area of application of the principle of personality is the humanization of working conditions. It is a permanent demand of Catholic social teaching that the individual must be able to develop his or her personal capabilities through his or her career and work position. It follows that the worker should not suffer mental and physical harm in the long run. For example, the assembly line cannot be regarded as the last word. True, one cannot just simply dismiss the laws of economic returns, but the dignity of the worker demands that labour should have priority over capital (cf. *Laborem Exercens*, No. 12), and this should be taken in account in the way in which business and economic structures are organized.

Freedom and responsibility are indivisibly bound up with the dignity of the human person which therefore demands that in the workplace the employee should be able to take a reasonable part in co-determination and responsibility. The Pope puts forward the socio-ethical demand that 'the human person can preserve his awareness of working "for himself" ' (*Laborem Exercens*, No. 15).

What the Church says

Second Vatican Council, Pastoral Constitution *Gaudium et Spes*

'The social order and its development must constantly yield to the good of the person, since the order of things must be subordinate to the order of persons and not the other way around, as the Lord suggested when he said that the Sabbath was made for man, and not man for the Sabbath' (No. 26).

The Pastoral Constitution deals with human dignity from Nos. 12 to 22 and with the human community from Nos. 23 to 32.

John XXIII, encyclical *Mater et Magistra*

'By the supreme law of this teaching [Catholic social teaching], man shall be the foundation, cause, and end of all social institutions ... This highest principle carries and protects the unassailable dignity of the human person' (No. 219 et seq.).

John Paul II, encyclical *Laborem Exercens*

'In fact, there is no doubt that human work has an ethical value of its own, which clearly and directly remains linked to the fact that the one who carries it out is a person, a conscious and free subject, that is to say a subject that decides about himself. This truth, which in a sense constitutes the fundamental and perennial heart of Christian teaching on human work, has had and continues to have primary significance for the formulation of the important social problems characterizing whole ages' (No. 6).

8. Solidarity or fraternity?
The person as a social being

The principle of personality should not be seen in isolation: it has an elemental counter-balancing relationship to the principle of solidarity. They inter-relate. If the one were to be regarded on its own, it would lead to an unsatisfactory and even dangerous individualism in the community, such as we witnessed, for instance, in the first stages of Europe's industrial development. On the other hand, were solidarity to be regarded by itself, it would lead to communal collectivism and ultimately – both for the individual and for social groupings – to unbearable curbs on freedom and self-determination. Such was the experience of Marxist-communist systems in the East.

For life in the community, for peaceful contact between different persons and for varied interest groups to function properly, the commitment of everyone to mutual solidarity is an indispensable duty. A community that does not have a minimum standard of commitment to mutual solidarity is not viable. Yet does it also need fraternity, brotherliness? Or are fraternity and solidarity one and the same?

The person as a social being

It was all put so very clearly in the account of the creation: 'So God created man in his own image; male and female he created them. And God blessed them, and God said to them, "Be fruitful, and multiply" ' (Gen. 1:27 et seq.). It is a basic fact of their existence that human beings are sexual creatures, seeking to complement themselves through the opposite sex and through human society. They are both capable of and in need of their complements.

By nature the human person is made to say 'thou'; that is, in the language of social philosophy, the person is a social being, an *ens sociale*. Only in meeting with the 'thou' in other people and in the community do they attain full development of their physical possibilities and personal gifts, as demonstrated by the hospital syndrome in deserted infants and in American experiments with rhesus monkeys. The small child that does not receive the necessary care, human attention and verbal communication falls behind in both physical and psychological development and can be damaged for life.

Every individual, especially the child, depends on the community for safety and personal development. There is no life without a family, no civil progress without the community. The progress of humanity is the result of the collective efforts and co-operation of many generations.

The basic law of social life

Social justice and peace in the community are based on the solidarity ties of the members of the community. Without social cohesion, the community lapses into separate groups and particular interests. Each person is indeed orientated towards the community; all rely on it for the security of their existence and for their individual development. We therefore need solidarity, which is the basic law of human life and of every society. Hence Catholic social teaching places the principle of solidarity beside the principle of personality. They stand in a complementary relationship to one another. We express this by saying: 'the human being is a person in community'. The individual acting in isolation from the community (like Robinson Crusoe) is a theory, a construct of the imagination.

The individual and the community, the person and society, are necessarily in a relationship of tension. On the one hand, we have the human person whose inalienable rights have such value that they cannot arbitrarily be subordinated to the communal interests or group egoism; while on the other hand, individual interests must not be pursued egoistically at the expense of the common good. The individual and society have an inescapable relationship of mutual commitment and responsibility. This basic law of society can be reduced to a simple formula: all for one, and one for all.

Liberalism claims that full realization of individual welfare will lead automatically to the highest possible level of common advantage. By contrast, collectivism seeks to prove that concentrating all the powers on the community can also bring about the maximum value to the individual. Both assumptions have been shown to be false.

Pluralism in the community

Pluralism in everyday life is an important and stimulating element of our free and democratic society. Those who decide on a free and open way of life must also approve of social variety and diversity of opinion, lifestyle and outlook. That implies commitment to mutual tolerance.

For many of our contemporaries this pluralism as such is a system of values and the central point of an emancipated, developed, higher quality of life. Yet it has no inherent value. It confers only the formal dimensions of an open space for different, differing and, indeed, competing value judgments and ways of life. Humanity cannot live by pluralism alone. Living in a pluralistic society presumes that the citizens themselves, and all the different groups in society, have convictions and values which enable them to pursue and fulfil their lives. A society that allows its convictions to be undermined in the name of pluralism and tolerance digs away at the very foundations on which it is built.

Furthermore, every community, including in particular one that is pluralistic needs a common basis of convictions, values and attitudes. If it does not have those, the centrifugal forces of pluralism will in the long run tear the community apart: because pluralism in itself has no power of integration.

Thinking in terms of competition

Modern industrial societies with their competitive market economies are without any doubt extremely productive. And yet the principle of competition is by itself not sufficient to meet the needs of a properly functioning industrial society.

A system based on the division of labour and competitiveness also has to depend on co-operation, which becomes distressingly plain in times of crisis when necessary actions in the interests of all fail because of self-interested group pressures. Liberal capitalism's idea of competition, like Marxist class attitudes, destroys the social body politic instead of drawing together all its strengths. The aim of Christian social reform is a social and economic order which builds on the co-operation and mutual help of all in solidarity with one another.

Fraternity instead of solidarity?

It is impossible nowadays to drown the call for brotherliness and community. Young people in particular, but not only they, seek to experience caring communities and alternative lifestyles. The protest inherent in this is directed at a de-personalized society where business is all. Human beings need room for manoeuvre in today's industrial societies with their blinkered emphasis on principles of competition and efficiency and their simultaneous tendencies to isolate individuals and to swamp them in the crowd. It would certainly be wrong to dismiss outright the principle of competition. The fact that achievement is part of the necessary inner structure of humanity is shown in the experience of performance and success in sport. But even so, human beings have a basic need for solidarity, community and fraternity.

A vast number of individuals and pressure groups, however, are striving for a reform of society that will lead to a fraternal world, a brotherly society of a common production, consumption and life. It poses the question whether fraternity is something different from, or more than, solidarity and whether, if it came to the push, the communal and social principle of solidarity could be replaced by fraternity.

The concept of fraternity comes, as the word itself denotes, from the family circle and signifies the particular blood bond of kinsfolk. Historically, the call from social reformers for a fraternal community has had (as written on countless banners) the goal of modelling society on the family. This aim was achieved once at least, when society was practically made up of family communities, that is of tribal units. In our highly-developed society, with its division of labour and complex inter-relationships, in the first place, the same thing is impossible and, in the second place, it is debatable whether anyone would really want it.

For behind any such demand there is basically a utopian view of society. Even references to kibbutzim in Israel and similar experiments do nothing to alter that. It is possible to achieve such social and economic organization in small communities and groups closely bound together by blood or ideology, but such experiences cannot be transferred to large industrial societies where people no longer feel themselves part of a family or ideological community. What has to, and should, be called for in its stead is a way of regulating society that permits and ensures that people can live and work together in solidarity and co-responsibility.

What the Church says

Second Vatican Council, Pastoral Constitution *Gaudium et Spes*

'But God did not create the human person alone; from the very beginning "man and woman he created them" (Gen. 1:27). Their bond constitutes the very first form of personal community. The human person is by his innermost nature a social being; without relationships to one another he can neither live nor create conditions for development' (No. 12).

'Man's social nature makes it evident that the progress of the human person and the advance of society itself hinge on each other. The beginning, the subject and the goal of all social institutions is and must be the human person, which for its part and by its very nature stands completely in need of social life' (No. 25).

The human community is dealt with in Nos. 23 to 32.

9. Who is responsible for the common good?

The principle of the common good is of fundamental importance for peaceful and prosperous life in the community. Wherever individuals and social groups follow only their own interests, life in the community is crippled at important points or the law of the jungle creeps in. For a peaceful and progressive development of the social body politic, the particular interests of the individual must be drawn to the common good of the whole community. In a free society this is a task not just for the state, though as the highest protector of the common good, the state does bear the ultimate responsibility.

The question of ultimate responsibility for the common good is of paramount importance in our modern industrial society and democratic mass communities. If all want to get the most for themselves and their interest groups from whatever the community can offer, who is going to ensure that justice and charity are available to all? The liberalism of early capitalism believed that the community would best be served if individuals worked to the best of their abilities for their own success. Today we know that is the case only in theory and in typically ideal circumstances. In practice it all looks very different. Opportunists and people living at society's expense, all trying to get the most out of the system, can render even the best institutions ineffective if there is nobody to put a stop to it in the interests of the common good. Our modern insurance and pensions systems can be seen as an example. If everyone wants to milk the cow and no one cares for it or feeds it, soon there will be no milk and the animal will die.

The state, guardian of the common good

We are accustomed to making the state responsible for the maintenance of the common good. And rightly so! Because this is the first and most important task of the state. In that lies the justification for its existence in the philosophy of law. Individuals and social groups on their own cannot satisfy or ensure all the necessities of life.

While in the past the state was expected above all to preserve the rule of law, to secure international peace and protection from foreign threat (the classical functions of government), the modern state is acquiring an ever greater responsibility for the common good in the social and economic field. A government today has to pursue properly planned policies, not only in times of crisis (though particularly then), in order to create the best possible economic and social conditions for its citizens. It has a further task in levelling out group pressures liable to upset the balance of democratic forces. The state has to balance the individual interests of the various and often competing interest groups and direct them towards the common good.

Group egoisms

Care for the common good is of particular significance in our pluralistic societies, where, because of a misinterpreted and excessive idea of freedom, personal interests and group egoisms threaten to undermine communities and institutions from the family right up to the state. Certainly, it is unreservedly true that the institutions exist for the people, not the people for the institutions. Social institutions, and among them the authorities too, have no purpose in themselves apart from the people for whom they have been created. Every social or economic association, such as a business, has a duty towards the people active in it. And so that the good of all (i.e., the common good) can be fully achieved, individual interests have to be subordinated to the general interest, and everything likely to harm the good of all has to be put aside. The common good comes before private gain! Modest demands of society and the renunciation of private gain, for example, are virtues that have long been regarded as outdated but of which we are sorely in need today.

However, the common good has to be reassessed if the elementary rights and needs of the individual are called into question. In particular cases it may be hard to decide between the rights of the individual and the interests of the community. One thinks, for instance, of air personnel staging a strike at peak holiday periods. In such cases the assertion of legitimate rights and demands can lead to a heavy burden on the public. The right to strike on the one hand, the common good on the other! It is easy to see to what extent group interests can call into question the common good.

The common responsibility of all

Today we cannot push on to the state alone the responsibility for the common good, because it is the common objective of every member of the social body politic. The trouble is that nowadays it is no longer a matter just of dealing with communities that are numerically small, relatively straightforward and easily supervised, but modern complex and anonymous mass societies. Anyone wanting to push sole responsibility for the common good on to the state in today's bureacratically administered societies, would in the long run end up with a ubiquitous welfare state.

To care for the comprehensive well-being of its citizens, the state and its institutions need to obtain a virtually untrammelled and, in the last instance, uncontrollable power over every individual. That can only be countered effectively if governmental tasks and responsibilities are confined to the minimum with as much authority as possible delegated to social institutions and organizations at lower levels according to the principle of subsidiarity. Of course this assumes the readiness of every individual and group to share in the responsibility for the common good, which means in effect modifying individual interests and desires.

In this context the initiatives of citizens and their care for the community are very much to be welcomed. Such group concerns (though often, sadly, egoistical) show a laudable readiness to act in the interests of the common good, particularly for environmental protection or other local needs. Nonetheless, we need legal frameworks to co-ordinate such activity more effectively and integrate it constructively into social planning. On the other hand, of course, it is intolerable if important plans, in the interests of the community, are thwarted for years by particular pressure groups.

Just how important the co-responsibility of society as a whole is for the common good is frequently demonstrated by economic crises. Government measures alone are not sufficient to get the ship afloat again. The government's economic policy can be undermined if strong social forces, such as the trade unions, are against it. The same goes for environmental protection policy. In such cases, too, the government must depend on the active co-operation of all citizens if there is to be improvement all along the line.

True democracy does not mean doing away with governmental activity in all sorts of fields without providing a substitute, as is indeed suggested from time to time, but that the people take responsibility themselves, or in association with social organizations, to do what is necessary. In good times and bad, a functioning democracy depends on the active co-operation of all its citizens. In that sense we can say that democracy means that all the people together bear responsibility for the common good.

The international common good

At this stage it is necessary to deal with the concerns of the common good internationally. The rich industrial nations cannot ignore a worldwide responsibility: an international common good does exist. After all, we are all in the same boat.

International ties of economic relations and the mutual dependence of all nations on earth have developed to such an extent that it is no longer possible for any state to pursue the interests of its society independently and uninfluenced by events in other countries. The superpowers are also dependent on international events, as was shown by the oil crisis. Help for the Third World is therefore anything but a matter of large-scale hand-outs. The international common good demands economic and political co-operation from all countries, rich or poor, to help solve the problems of the future.

What the Church says

John XXIII, encyclical *Mater et Magistra*

'The common good includes the embodiment of that prerequisite for society which enables or facilitates the full development of men's potential' (No. 65).

Second Vatican Council, Pastoral Constitution *Gaudium et Spes*

'Men, families and the various groups which make up the civil community are aware that they cannot achieve a truly human life by their own unaided efforts. They see the need for a wider community within which each one makes his specific contribution every day towards an ever broader realization of the common good. For this purpose they set up a political community which takes various forms. The political community exists consequently for the sake of the common good, in which it finds its full justification and significance and the source of its inherent legitimacy. Indeed, the common good embraces the sum of those conditions of the social life whereby men, families and associations more adequately and readily may attain their own perfection' (No. 74).

10. Social justice or social love?

Any Christian who becomes active in politics is faced with the question of whether it is going to be enough to work for social justice in the general sociological sense or whether the gospel demands more. The ultimate social principle, to which the gospel of Christ commits us, is that we love our neighbour as ourselves. What relationship is there between social justice and social love? In the gospel sense, can one turn love into a social principle?

Justice is the highest principle of every reasonable social order. Yet anyone committed to the teachings of the gospel has to ask whether justice is enough as the highest social principle, or whether Christian teaching does not have to call on the gospel's highest principle, charity, or to put it better, the *agape* of the New Testament, in order to remain true to its mission. Christ sent out the disciples to serve the people selflessly with the command: 'A new commandment I give to you, that you love one another; even as I have loved you, that you also love one another' (John 13:34).

As a political goal, is it enough for the Christian simply to pursue social justice? That is, should the Christian seek justice in a legal, business and secular manner? Or should the highest principle be love?

The social principle of justice

Justice as a social principle is self-explanatory. It is obvious that any communal or economic order can only be described as 'social' if human rights are respected. What justice demands, however, is a matter on which disagreement is possible. For example, where exactly does the truth lie in settling wage levels in labour disputes or determining how long the working week should be? The principle of justice does not provide a comprehensive yardstick that can be used in each specific case. In the final analysis, what is just can only be discovered from the actual circumstances involved, the current laws in force and from basic human rights. Granted that, however, is it enough that I as a Christian give my neighbour only what I am bound to do in justice or in law? Does not the gospel demand more?

An obligation to love?

This brings us to the question whether love can be regarded as a social principle in its own right, in other words as a structural principle for maintaining economic and political life. To put it more precisely: can or should one strive for an economic order that demands mutual love of people rather than relationships of justice? One does not generally think of it in that way because 'love' is not normally part of the vocabulary of the social sciences, unless as a socio-ethical appeal or as a motivation to social action. Besides which, love is usually assigned the specific field of organized charity.

It is important that we look at this clearly. Love cannot, and should not, be a (cheap) surrogate for the justice that is owed but denied. It is most emphatically not the job of charity to cover the shortcomings of justice with the mantle of love, as was rightly made very clear by Pius XI in his encyclical *Quadragesimo Anno* (No. 137, 4).

On the other hand, love is a fundamental principle in the papal social teachings put forward in the encyclicals. It should play the 'chief role' in establishing the new order of society, as laid down in the same encyclical (No. 137); it should be its 'soul' and 'supreme law'.

Justice and love

It is remarkable that justice and love are often mentioned in the same breath as the most important guiding principles. In the social encyclicals they are corresponding concepts, often a matching pair. They are put forward as the basic principles for a correct social and economic order, in which justice 'permeates governmental and social institutions completely' and in which love is 'the soul of the order' (*Quadragesimo Anno*, No. 88). Many similar texts could be quoted.

This dual foundation of social teaching on justice and love as social principles begins to make complete sense when one considers that papal social teaching acknowledges that for the long-term restructuring of society, it is necessary to reform conditions as well as mentality and morals (*Quadragesimo Anno*, No. 77). When the encyclical was first published the insistence on moral reform and reassessment of attitudes drew mild amusement and dismissive remarks about social romanticism. Today we know better. Now we tend to speak, however, of 'change in awareness and relationships' instead of change in mentality and of 'changing the structures or systems' instead of the reform of conditions.

We have learned in the meantime that a real reform of society is not possible without change in social relationships and ways of thinking. Marx's economic determinism, assuming automatic changes in human social relationships from changes in the economic structure, has been shown to be utterly wrong. More and more we gather, even from Marxist critics of the system and neo-Marxist theorists that new (communist) man is not the automatic product of revised economic relationships of production. A so-called change in consciousness must be active and contemporaneous if reforms are to have a lasting effect.

Love as a social principle

We now have to ask ourselves what particular tasks love as a social principle can have if it is to be more than just a charitable mantle for social and economic policy.

1. Social love rises above the demand for justice. This is of great importance because experience has taught us that justice is not enough to achieve a world that is really worthy of humanity. A social order regulated solely on the principle of justice does not go far enough to meet the demand of being worthy of humanity, even though it may go a long way towards it. The highest and ultimate Christian goal is a community based on solidarity and fraternity in

85

society and the economy, which cannot be forced by legislation; it is necessary to use other means, that is, the social power of love.

But quite beyond that, selfless love and brotherliness are needed to bring about the realization of the demands of justice, because natural means alone would not suffice. The Second Vatican Council said, for instance, that lasting peace among nations is in the last resort the outcome of love that goes further than anything justice can achieve (*Gaudium et Spes*, No. 78). Something we have to call to mind time and again is that to establish justice in this world there must be people prepared to devote themselves selflessly to others and to building a juster society.

2. Social love is a communicative and integrative force. However perfect the social order, it cannot create a living community from the sum total of individuals, organizations and institutions. True, such a social order is a necessary condition, but not the ultimate goal. Justice can control whatever causes social conflict but it cannot force people together. Every community, every society, needs a common bond. The communicative and integrative force is love.

3. Social love is also a principle of structure. Love is not something to be laid down by law but there are ways and means of regulating society that strengthen the principle of human solidarity and brotherliness. As a structural principle for promoting social and economic order, love means that both the models of unlimited competition and of the Marxist class struggle are excluded from the Christian view of humanity. Social love points positively in the direction of a social model in which all those who take part in the process of production are brought together with equal rights in a co-operative system.

4. Social love has an eschatological-revolutionary power. By its very nature love is total, dedicated to the absolute, knowing no boundaries or conditions. In this it possesses revolutionary power which not only calls into question but also threatens to destroy the existing order. It is not satisfied with what has already been achieved, not even in the social and economic field. It strives to overcome individual self-seeking and group egoism and to break up hardened attitudes. In the sure knowledge that the eschatological

kingdom has already begun through Jesus Christ, social love has the revolutionary power to overcome all barriers and to seek entirely new ways of doing things. And that is exactly what the world expects of Christians.

What the Church says

Pius XI, encyclical *Quadragesimo Anno*

'But in effecting all this, the law of charity, "which is the bond of perfection", must always take a leading role. How completely deceived, therefore, are those rash reformers who concern themselves with the enforcement of justice alone – and this, commutative justice – and in their pride reject the assistance of charity! Admittedly, no vicarious charity can substitute for justice which is due as an obligation and is wrongfully denied. Yet even supposing that everyone should finally receive all that is due to him, the widest field for charity will always remain open. For justice alone can, if faithfully observed, remove the causes of social conflict but can never bring about union of minds and hearts' (No. 137).

11. Humanity's responsibility towards its Creator

Freedom and responsibility regarding the creation

This chapter deals with two aspects of the Christian picture of humanity: its freedom and its existence as a created being. They determine the Christian's relationship to the creation and hence to current environmental questions. As God's creation, humanity is not only part of nature, but also responsible towards the Creator for the way it deals with nature. The gift of freedom imposes simultaneously a task and a responsibility.

The human race was created by God: this is the inescapable basis of the Christian view of humanity. The scriptures make this basic truth evident from their very earliest pages. This Christian view does not permit humanity merely to look at itself, but directs its view 'above', to the basic source, beyond humanity itself, of authority for human behaviour. Human beings cannot thank themselves for their existence, but a Power that stands above them; and in the final analysis, they are not responsible to themselves but to the Hand from which they sprung. What consequences arise for Catholic social teaching from this transcendental destiny and humanity's responsibility towards its Creator?

Humanity is not a law unto itself

According to the Christian view, the world is not at humankind's sole disposal. Human beings may not do everything that it lies in their power to do, because they are bound by an eternal law above them and independent of their decisions. They shape their own world, it is true, but they did not create it. Human schemes and intentions have before them this internal law which the Creator has built into the world's structures and the human race. The world is not, in the Christian understanding, something that happened by chance but a carefully planned and designed order, and it is up to humanity to regulate within this God-created order its own world and its own life. It is always bound to this divine basic order and God's eternal law. The Ten Commandments embody a code for living which human beings cannot infringe without paying a price.

Opium of the people

Karl Marx attributed the religious alienation of the people, as he expressed it, to humanity's religious ties with a God who is above and independent of the world. Humanity cannot be itself as long as it has an obligation to this external law. Religious alienation prevents human beings from devoting themselves entirely to their own concerns and from changing their world. As Marx put it, religion is the opium of the people, consoling them with promises of a better life hereafter and so preventing them from defending themselves against their fate and from changing the inhuman living conditions in which they are enslaved.

But for Christians, awareness of the transcendental element in life is the basis of true freedom, because it makes them internally free from the world's shortcomings and opens a new horizon to life itself. Knowledge of the meaning of creation and human life makes them aware that effort to give human dignity to the social order is reasonable and is not in vain. The fact that the human being is God's creation does not stop Christians from tackling, with determination and creative joy, the task of restructuring social relationships and making the world a better place. The Christian knows that he or she has been specifically commissioned by the Creator to 'subdue' the earth and to 'till it and keep it' (Gen. 1:28; 2:15).

Having been given this assignment, humanity is obliged to render account to the Creator. It is therefore quite out of the question for the Christian simply to let things slide and await the hereafter. The very opposite is the case!

The responsibility of freedom

In contrast to the animals, directed by instinct, human beings have been created with the power to make their own free decisions. This freedom is God's gift but it means responsibility. Humanity may be called to freedom, but it carries full responsibility for what it makes of itself and of the world. Freedom is bound up with responsibility, and one influences the other. Human beings are responsible for the world, for maintaining the environment, for humane living and working conditions.

Technology, means of transport, the economy, etc., are in themselves neither good nor bad. True enough, the scriptures lay down that everything that God has created is good by its very nature: the disorder arose from the human race. Because they are free, men and women can transmute original blessing into curse. If technical and civilizing progress threatens to turn into a Moloch that devours everything in its path then it is people who have sinned, not the technology or other outward trappings. The economy does not violate humanity; it is humanity that permits inhuman economic structures.

Humanity must have a responsible approach to its freedom. There is no freedom without ties, without recognition of its limits. The dilemma facing our Western civilization is particularly noticeable when it comes to the understanding of freedom. Our contemporary civilization seems to have arrived at a point where it is clearly not in a position to act with the necessary decisiveness to lay down limits to the use of freedom. Freedom without commitment to social order, in other words the indiscriminate use of freedom is self-destructive. That every such abuse in some way or other ends up in loss of freedom has been shown all too often in human history. Freedom must be accountable.

Responsibility for creation

The creation is included in humanity's responsibility towards its Creator. God has made the creation freely available to humanity, so that it is responsible for what it freely makes out of it. Abuse of freedom brings fearful vengeance. Humanity in destroying nature destroys its own living space.

Nature, the creation, is not totally at human disposal. It is and remains God's property and has only been granted to humanity for a limited period: 'The Lord God took the man and put him in the garden of Eden to till it and keep it' (Gen. 2:15). It says nothing here about damaging, destroying, or plundering.

For Catholic theology and the Catholic understanding of the world, it is inconceivable that the human race can do with the world as it wishes. What characterizes Catholic thought is that the earth remains the Creator's property and that humanity is his guest. The earth has been given to human beings to live in, but one day they have to give it back to God the Creator and answer for their use of it.

This responsibility is made very clear when God calls Adam to account: 'cursed is the ground because of you' (Gen. 3:17). The earth bears the curse of thorns and thistles not because of itself but because of what Adam did. We are responsible for the earth and what we do with it. The creation is fatally bound to humanity – and the other way round.

A fatal misunderstanding

It is claimed that Western humanity has exploited the earth and robbed it of its resources, because it was laid down in Gen. 1:28: 'fill the earth, and subdue it; and have dominion over the fish of the sea, and over the birds of the air, and over every living thing that moves upon the earth.' Hence, the threat to the ecological balance is regarded as the outcome of the Christian teaching about the creation.

This is a fatal misunderstanding. It has been explained before that in these pages we seek to say something about humanity's spiritual destiny, giving a reply to the basic question: what is humanity? The reply is that humankind has been placed over the whole of creation, it is the image of God, that is, God's partner (Gen. 1:27).

Awareness of the fact that the creation is God's work, given to humanity allowed people in the Bible freedom to use the world in the building up of their societies – a world no longer the playground of demonic forces but something well created, entrusted to human beings and one day to be restored to God. That one should destroy nature or plunder the planet is unimaginable. Yet there is the additional issue that people have long held the belief that the earth's resources are inexhaustible and that the human race can do the planet no harm. Modern technology and science have changed all that. It makes our responsibility for the creation all the greater.

What the Church says

German Bishops' Conference, Declaration on Environmental Questions and Energy Supplies entitled *The future of creation – future of mankind (1980)*

'The world is God's gift to humanity, given to humanity to pass on. Man therefore has responsibility for the generations that come after him. In this way the creation becomes an inheritance which each generation owes to the one that comes after it and which it cannot consume away or burden with intolerable mortgages . . .

'We are not creators, but the created. To seek to be lords over all, as God is, is the origin of sin. We cannot start from nothing to attain our desires and wishes without limit. For us freedom means accepting that freedom and using it with the conditions attached to it. The Creator gives us a share in his creative freedom. We must have the courage to develop this. That presupposes the courage to accept and receive it as the gift of God. There is a spirituality in the Christian relationship to the world that arises from the basic slogan: "Acceptance and response" ' (II,5; III,1).

12. Christian utopia or Christian realism?

The existence of sin determines very definitely the Christian under-standing of humanity and therefore also Catholic social teaching. In the biblical view, the human being is an ambivalent creature, lastingly stamped in the very core by the liability to sin. 'Christian realism' takes humanity as it really is: by nature neither exclu-sively good nor bad. Socio-ethical realism is also a characteristic strain of Catholic social teaching, rejecting social utopianism in all its forms.

The existence of sin

The first two chapters of the creation story give a thoroughly optimistic view of humanity living in harmony with itself and its surroundings, yet the chapters that follow paint dark pictures of the human liability to temptation and sin. The original harmony does not last, paradise is destroyed by human beings themselves.

These two views have a dialectical relationship. They are not diametrically opposed, but each qualifies the other. This double character is basic to the biblical understanding of humanity and, from the Christian point of view, the picture is ambivalent, neither solely optimistic nor solely pessimistic. It would be unbiblical and unrealistic to interpret humanity in a one-sidedly idealistic way on the basis of the first two chapters of scripture and not to take seriously the human failings and social contradictions dealt with in the chapters that follow.

Christian revelation does not idealize human beings but regards them seriously in the greatness and dignity given them by God, and in the fact that their behaviour can be questionable and contradic-tory. This revelatory truth is the basis of Catholic social teaching. The Christian view of humanity accepts people realistically as they present themselves in their historical ambivalence. It is in this connection that we speak of 'Christian realism'.

93

The origins of evil

It is important for the Christian understanding of humanity to seek the origin of evil from which this ambivalence springs. The Christian holds that the source lies in people themselves and not outside. Human beings are ultimately not the product of their environment even though it may influence their way of life and their desires. The origin of evil is indissolubly linked with human freedom and cannot be put aside without rejecting that freedom.

For Karl Marx and his materialistic philosophy, evil originates in economic relations, not in the people themselves. The human being is the result of the relationships of production, and therefore fundamentally changing those will also change human beings and their social behaviour. We know, however, that this is not true, since evil's origin lies more deeply: in people themselves. Hence every social reform must begin with the human being and be accompanied by inner conversion, the biblical *metanoia*.

And there is something else to bear in mind. The efficacy of evil is not something accidental, but an existentially permanent stigma of the human race throughout history. For that reason human contradictions, both individually and historically, can never be completely solved; which is why social reform will always be an ongoing task for humanity.

Marx-Christ

The parallel between the Christian and Marxist understanding of history is no accident; both are directed, in a linear manner, towards an eschatological (future) completion.

The Christian revelation has history starting with its original state in paradise, destroyed by the human lapse into sin. Christ comes to save humanity by making it new through baptism. The release of people from sin and evil is a creative act by God. As a result Christ's redeeming act, both the human race and the entire cosmos are moving to their definitive eschatological fulfilment, which God himself will conclude with an act of new creation.

The Marxist view, too, looks back to an ideal first state, the original communist society. For Karl Marx the fall from grace is the introduction of private property and the rise of the class society. Humanity will be freed through abolition of private ownership of the means of production, automatically transforming the people and the community (the social superstructure). At the end of a certain period of transition the new society will have achieved perfect communism.

The fundamental difference between these two ideas of history lies in the fact that, in the Christian concept, human redemption (liberation) and the attainment of God's kingdom presuppose human co-operation, while, in the Marxist concept, liberation (abolition of private property) is the work of humanity alone. The 'redemption' or rather self-redemption, occurs here and now. Humanity creates its own paradise, in fact on this earth. For Karl Marx the lapse into sin (evil) is merely an event in history, the result simply of social relationships, not something that has struck humanity in the innermost core of its being. It need hardly be said what a disastrous effect this Marxist interpretation of history and the human race has had on world events.

Christian realism

Differences in outlook are to a considerable extent a battle between views of humanity. When one considers that every social policy and system has at its heart a definite picture of the human race, it becomes clear that the 'battle for people's minds' is of global importance for everyday life and is not just egghead wrangling.

The Enlightenment view of humanity and society, responsible for producing both the optimism of Rousseau and the pessimism of Hobbes, still has much influence today. With its long-held and uninterrupted faith in progress, the optimistic viewpoint has in general tended to prevail: it is only in our own day that the mirror has been broken.

Because of the Christian view it holds of humanity, Catholic social teaching has always been sceptical of an uncritically euphoric view of progress such as was current during the Enlightenment. However, a one-sided pessimistic scepticism regarding humanity, its possibilities and its perspectives regarding the future is unchristian, too. Sometimes it looks as if the present day optimism about progress will simply keel over into a post-Enlightenment pessimism.

Also the various theories of environmental influence, which regard people as more or less the product of their surroundings, put blinkers on the true picture of humanity, because they either grant too small a role to the power of freedom of personal decision and individual responsibility or they deny them a role at all.

The Christian view of humanity looks at human ambivalence and the fractures in human nature seriously, but it takes into account humanity's ability to control nature in accordance with the rules laid down by the Creator and with a sense of responsibility towards the creation, and to carry creation forward on the way to fulfilment.

Christian utopianism?

It has become fashionable to speak of a Christian utopia or a 'real utopia'. Looked at superficially, it is not always clear what all this means. If this way of thinking is based on the fulfilment of God's kingdom at the end of time and the Messiah's everlasting empire of peace, we have to bear in mind that this goal of salvation does not lie in the power of human beings but is solely the work of God. It cannot therefore be used to measure contemporary social policy.

If, however, the Christian 'real utopia' is taken to mean the duty of Christians to play a part now in bringing about God's kingdom in this world, then we have to deal with a task which is an absolute imperative for us. Catholic social teaching's view of humanity is always realistic: it takes the fractured condition of human nature seriously but leaves room for humanity's opportunity to accept God's offer and to be led by him to the liberty of the children of God.

What the Church says

Pius XII, *Christmas address 23 December 1956*

'He [the human being] is capable of doing good, but also evil, capable of realizing all the positive possibilities and talents of his nature or of placing them in danger. Because of the great values at stake, which in the 20th century have taken on a tremendous dimension, this very risk creates and underlies the fearful paradox facing our contemporaries. There is no other means of salvation to overcome this except the return to true realism, which with equal certainty encompasses not only the dignity of mankind but also its limitations – its ability to overcome them, and the reality of sin.'

Paul VI, encyclical *Octogesima Adveniens*

'Today the weaknesses of ideologies are better perceived through the concrete systems in which they are trying to affirm themselves. Bureaucratic socialism, technocratic capitalism, and authoritarian democracy are showing how difficult it is to solve the great human problem of living together in justice and equality. How in fact could they escape the materialism, egoism, or constraint which inevitably go with them? This is the source of a protest which is springing up more or less everywhere, as a sign of deep-seated sickness, while at the same time we are witnessing the rebirth of what it is agreed to call "utopias". These claim to resolve the political problem of modern societies better than the ideologies. It would be dangerous to disregard this. The appeal to a utopia is often a convenient excuse for those who wish to escape from concrete tasks in order to take refuge in an imaginary world. (To live in a hypothetical future is a facile alibi for rejecting immediate responsibilities.) But it must be clearly recognized that this kind of criticism of existing society often provokes the forward-looking imagination both to perceive in the present the disregarded possibility hidden within it, and to direct itself towards a fresh future' (No. 37).

PART TWO

Economic and social order from the Christian point of view

Catholic social teaching, as an integral part of the Church's message, lays down socio-ethical rules for economic life and for the structuring of the economic order. It is not to be compared with a textbook on economics. The Church holds the view that the study of economic laws and the inter-relationship of economic phenomena are not within its competence which concerns matters of faith.

It *is*, however, the Church's task to proclaim ethical fundamentals for economic life and the world of work in order to ensure that the economy is so ordered that it meet the demands of human dignity and social justice. Using these as guidelines, it tests existing economic relationships and exposes possible infringements of human dignity and the rights of working people and offences against the moral order.

At the same time the Church's social message puts forward, in accordance with these basic rules, suggestions of new ways to solve social problems and to promote the further development of the social order. It points to possible directions in which to seek the realization of a socially just organization of economic life.

The laws of economics confine themselves to procedures and sets of circumstances, establishing why things happen in the economy and what consequences arise from certain economic relationships for particular firms or the economy as a whole. Knowledge of economic laws enables the expert to analyse the origins of malfunctions and devise corrective measures, looking ahead to future expansion. The specifically human goals in the economy play no part in these laws, for which reason they might be judged to be neutral values. How the economy works and what ethical rules it should follow in its structure are matters for socio-economic policy. It is precisely here that the Church, with its particular competence, is called to be the people's advocate and the guardian of human dignity. To exercise these functions properly we come back to the socio-ethical rules which Catholic social teaching has in the course of time formulated as the very basis of the Christian understanding of humanity and which the Church has proclaimed in its social messages. An example of this is John Paul II's encyclical on work, *Laborem Exercens*.

The aim of this introduction is to present a general overview of Catholic economic ethics. It lays down the most important socio-ethical fundamentals of Catholic social teaching and will set out to explain clearly where that teaching stands today in questions of economics and the world of work, and what options there are in the various economic models arising from socialist and capitalist thought. It will not and cannot give a creative overview of all the questions related to economics. Some important areas have to be excluded, for instance, questions about the international economic order and the politics of development or the complexities of labour market policy.

1. Is there a Catholic economic order?

At the start of every debate about economic affairs, when it comes from the Church and at the behest of its teaching authority, there is always the question whether the Church indeed has any originating jurisdiction in this field. For that matter, how far does gospel responsibility extend over economic life? It is already known that the scriptures contain no direct guidance for contemporary industrial matters. We have to begin by saying that Jesus proclaimed the coming of the kingdom; he did not deal in detail with questions involving the economic order. We have already cleared up this complex question in Part One in the chapter 'What authority has the Church in economic and social questions?' The first chapter in this section sets out to expand on what has already been said.

The question is often asked what a Catholic economic order should look like. Such a question can be understood in a proper manner, but the way it is put is wrong. For it would be incorrect to assume that there is something worked out to the last detail that can be called a definitely 'Catholic' economic order, quite different from every other. It is correct, however, to put the question if it seeks solutions to economic problems according to Christian principles and socio-ethical standards.

No economic textbook

It would be wrong to compare Catholic social teaching to a textbook on economics: there is no such thing as a Catholic national economy. At best, the Church could give guidance based on the socio-ethical principles of social teaching. The Church has only a limited jurisdiction over economic questions. Its teaching authority is confined to matters of faith and morals. For that reason it cannot

give binding and detailed prescriptions for an economic order –
even to Christians.

The Church's task, based on the mission entrusted to it by Jesus
Christ, is to lay down principles and socio-ethical standards for a
social economy that respects human rights, prevents infringements
of human dignity in economic life and co-operates in the progressive humanization of the world of work.

It should never be forgotten that the Christian revelation contains
no concrete and specific economic order; the economy is not the
direct concern of the message of salvation. The scriptures have no
indications or statements which must lead with absolute necessity
to a *wholly worked out* social and economic order. That is not to
say the Christian message is indifferent to social life and economic
structures. On the contrary, where Christ's gospel is lived out to
the full, it must inevitably have an effect on the world of work and
economic relations, even though the scriptures do not prescribe a
fixed economic order binding on all.

The autonomy of the economic realm

The Church recognizes the autonomy of economic life: it claims
no teaching authority in questions of economics as a science and
problems of a technical nature (*Quadragesimo Anno*, Nos. 41 and
42). The Second Vatican Council has emphatically admitted the
'autonomy of earthly realities' and expressed regret over mistakes
it has made in this field in the past, such as for instance in the case
of Galileo (*Gaudium et Spes*, No. 36).

Catholic social teaching has taken as its starting point that it first
of all has the task of establishing principles for an economic life
worthy of human dignity and socially just. It has not been granted
particular jurisdiction over specialist questions of economics; it is
much more a matter of respecting the judgments of economic
science. It is unavoidable, however, that tensions arise between
what is needed from a socio-ethical point of view and what is
economically effective. However regrettable, there are no absolute
priorities here. When it comes down to it, what is desirable socio-
ethically has to be weighed against what is possible economically:
there would quickly be trouble if one discarded basic economic

laws. Miracles, in the sense of simply ignoring natural laws, do not happen in economic life.

From the above it is clear that Catholic social teaching is basically open to differing solutions of social and economic problems. In each individual case it has to be gauged how socio-ethical principles can best be applied with economic effectiveness. Varying conditions may lead to quite different decisions and yet be based on the same ethical ground rules. To take a position of principle regarding a specific economic system is not possible on the basis only of Catholic social teaching.

Humanity at the centre

This basic openness to a variety of possible solutions should not be confused with a rudderless desire for popularity. Even though the scriptures contain no specific teaching on economics or the social order, the integrated picture of humanity and the world in revelation excludes certain definite social and economic structures, and the Christian view of humanity also presents very firm guidelines concerning every aspect of social and economic life. In this connection it is necessary to recall Catholic social principles and the way they work.

Among the basic principles of economic ethics is the affirmation that humanity is 'the originator, core and goal of all economics' (*Gaudium et Spes*, No. 63) and that labour has priority over capital (*Laborem Exercens*, No. 12). Economic development must always come from the human being as its source and its subject, and economic planning always has to work for human needs, fears and hopes, because only the human being can be the ultimate goal of the economy. The thesis that humanity must be the focal point of the world of work and the economy (anthropocentrism) is formulated not in the sense of presenting a specific model, but as a general proviso for overall economic policy.

Capital and labour

Of basic importance to Catholic social teaching is the axiom that as factors of production capital and labour both carry equal weight and are inter-dependent. As long ago as 1891, the encyclical *Rerum Novarum* stated that 'capital can exist without labour as little as labour can exist without capital' (No. 15). An economic system that is socially just has to start out from this fundamental concept and seek to attain the best possible co-operation of both factors. How that is to be achieved in individual cases must depend on circumstances and cannot be subjected to hard and fast rules.

This does not do away with all the conflicts of interest between capital and labour, but Catholic social teaching rejects the idea of the class war as a matter of principle. And if it has to be said here that the two factors of production carry equal weight, that does not mean in any way that they both enjoy the same ethical value. The personal factor of labour has, in accordance with the clear proclamation of the encyclical *Laborem Exercens*, a socio-ethical precedence over capital. In cases of conflict, in other words, if the fundamental rights of the workers are concerned, their personal needs are not simply to be subordinated to the economic laws of profitability.

The social market economy

In many ways the concept of the 'social market economy' undoubtedly comes close to the basic needs of Catholic social teaching, but it cannot be regarded as a Catholic economic concept. As has already been shown, no definite economic order can be held to be Catholic because it is not the task of social teaching to establish a specific order. Nonetheless, nothing prevents the realization of the goals of Catholic social teaching and its economic principles through the concept of the social market economy.

That must mean, however, that such an economic order really justifies and deserves the prefix *'social'*, and that this does not provide the excuse for ruthless economic tactics. Not everything that is praised as social market economy is worthy of the name. Very often all such talk is merely camouflage for opposing socio-political reforms and an easy way of soothing the social conscience.

What the Church says

Second Vatican Council, *Pastoral Constitution Gaudium et Spes*

'In the socio-economic realm, too, the dignity and total vocation of the human person must be honoured and advanced along with the welfare of society as a whole. For man is the source, the centre, and the purpose of all socio-economic life.

'Hence, numerous reforms are needed at the socio-economic level, along with universal changes in ideas and attitudes. Now in this area the Church maintains certain principles of justice and equity as they apply to individuals, societies, and international relations. In the course of the centuries and with the light of the gospel she has worked out these principles as right reason demanded. In modern times, especially, the Church has enlarged upon them' (No. 63).

Instruction of the Congregation for the Doctrine of the Faith, *22 March 1986*

'The principles referred to lay the foundations for criteria to assess social situations, structures and systems. In this way the Church does not hesitate to denounce living conditions that offend against the dignity and freedom of human beings ... These criteria also affect economic, social and political systems. The social teaching of the Church prescribes no system, but makes allowance for recognising all in the light of its own basic principles, to the extent that these systems meet or fail to meet the demands of human dignity' (No. 74).

2. From class struggle to class integration

In our pluralistic society, Catholic social teaching has to compete with other ideas on how things should be run. It has to oppose different concepts and maintain itself against economic strategies which will in part have conflicting starting points. It is therefore sensible to explain first of all the basic concepts of Catholic social teaching. This will also answer the question as to what is the key for solving actual contemporary social problems and for a forward-looking perspective for shaping our economic order.

Questions about the further development of our economic and social systems are being raised today for all sorts of reasons. In part, this comes from those who, for whatever reason, are not happy with what they see in our current economic situation and, on the other hand, from those who, on the basis of their social responsibility, seek to work out the perspectives of future social and economic policy. The extraordinarily rapid changes in our 'computer age' call for constant reassessment of changing economic and social relationships. It is only natural that this also calls into question the contribution and future perspectives of Catholic social teaching, and this cannot be answered without knowledge and understanding of its basic principles and what it regards as its goals.

It can therefore be taken for granted that, because of its biblical origin and theological nature, this social teaching cannot and does not want to produce a different economic system. As has already been said, it is no detailed textbook for a so-called Catholic economy. What concerns it is conversion of the biblical and religious message of the Old and New Testaments into the reality of economic and social life. True, in this message there are socio-ethical principles and an unalterably Christian view of humanity and society which may not satisfy the urge for order and structure with a unitary draft or design for shaping community and social policy, but it can and does lay down basic directions and excludes some specific concepts.

Integration of the working class

Seeking perspectives for the further development of our economic order means believing in the need for, and capacity for, improvement in our system. It has become the fashion, particularly among the younger generation, to speak about the basic inability of established systems to react positively to new social circumstances and draw up constructive designs for the future. The Marcuse approach of 'one-dimensional man' has become a substitute gospel for many. This pessimism concerning politics, society and human culture contradicts the New Testament message of hope and is never shared by Catholic social pronouncements.

Since its origins in the first half of the 19th century, i.e., since the so-called 'social question' arose, Catholic social teaching has worked uninterruptedly for developing a just social and economic order. In the course of its efforts, amid constantly changing basic conditions, it has shown the capacity to adapt even when developments were stormy. Its basic principle and clarity about its goal has remained constant in all these years: getting rid of the class struggle by integrating the working class into the whole community.

In the 19th century there was talk for a long time about the formation of the proletariat as a specific class. This was meant to express the feeling that it should be a goal of social policy to incorporate the emerging sector of the workers, which had come into being through the new industrial processes, into economic and social bodies as an equal partner. In other words, the class struggle would be overcome by integrating the working class into the community.

Renunciation of Marxism

What has just been said about the fundamentals of Catholic social teaching means the unequivocal and irrevocable renunciation of Marxism. The Marxist ideal is based on acceptance of a class society determined by capitalism; overcoming this is possible only through class struggle with the aim of abolishing private ownership of the means of production. The collectivization to follow is in the Marxist view necessary to achieve the social revolution. At the end of the revolutionary struggle the abolition of the class society will ensue and the means of production will pass into the hands of the workers. This will end once and for all the 'enslavement' of the workers who then become the subject of economic processes.

The reality of socialism looks very different. That is generally recognized. Quite rightly John Paul II makes clear in *Laborem Exercens* that 'in dialectical materialism, too, man is not in the first instance the embodiment of labour and the source of effectiveness in the processes of production; on the contrary, he is seen to be, and is treated, as dependent on matter' (No. 13).

A little later the Pope makes it clear that desirable social reforms can hardly be brought about automatically by the abolition of private ownership of the means of production because that only means that ownership passes from one group to another, in other words, to the party or state apparatus, without the workers gaining any control (No. 14).

On these and other grounds the fact that in the West and in the Third World there are many Christians ready to avail themselves of the Marxist analysis is not without dangers. Without fully realizing it, they often adopt, together with the analysis of society, the ideas of how to solve its problems: namely, the class struggle and the abolition of private property by violence, with the establishment of a communist society thereby.

Co-determination and co-ownership

Catholic social teaching is quite different. It believes that class conflict can be overcome by industrial co-determination and economic co-ownership. In contrast to the Marxist thesis, its premise is that class antagonism and the opposition of capital to labour do not arise from the economic system but from false thinking and mistaken ways of treating people, which is exactly what the Pope says in *Laborem Exercens* (No. 13). According to the clear and consistent traditional teaching of the social encyclicals, capital and labour belong together and have equal importance as being indispensable to the industrial process (*Rerum Novarum*, No. 15 and *Quadragesimo Anno*, No. 53). The vision of this teaching is that the task of social policy is to link labour and capital in a co-operative system so that, as partners with equal rights, they can work together in the best possible way for the common good.

In the early days of the Catholic social movement, it was believed that social questions could be solved by forming production co-operatives, that is, setting up worker-owned industrial enterprises on the basis of contracts of co-operation. Some bishops also sympathized with this idea, but the ideals did not live up to the reality. All such attempts rapidly came to grief for a variety of economic and human reasons. Quite soon thoughts turned to integrating the workers into industrial enterprise as equal partners through co-determination and as shareholders in the firm they work for. This goal has not been given up to the present day. It plays an important role in the Pope's basic reflections in his encyclical on human work (No. 14).

Where the problems lie

The communal perspectives of Catholic social teaching proclaim: no abolition of private property, but the sharing by all in the means of production; no class struggle, but co-operation between capital and labour on the basis of co-determination and co-ownership.

The democratization of the industrial process by co-determination, however, comes up against very difficult economic boundaries. If a company is to remain viable, it cannot do away with effective structures for making decisions. A system of parliamentary democracy can hardly be transferred into the industrial field. Workers' participation without doubt is a very worthwhile aim, but how much is the individual employee to carry the burden of risk-taking? Above all: do workers themselves wish to have this kind of participation? Many are more interested in what they can take home through fatter wage packets and shares in the firm's profits than in ownership rights which cannot always be realized. Co-ownership in the firm tends to inhibit financial flexibility and, for that matter, worker mobility. People with a stake in the firm cannot all that easily quit their jobs and take their share with them. There are still a lot of problems to solve before a satisfactory form of industrial co-ownership can be introduced.

What the Church says

Pius XI, encyclical *Quadragesimo Anno*

'For if the class struggle abstains from enmities and mutual hatred, it gradually changes into an honest discussion of differences founded on a desire for justice, and if this is not that blessed peace for which we all seek, it can and ought to be the point of departure from which to move forward to the mutual co-operation of the Industries and Professions' (No. 114).

John Paul II, encyclical *Laborem Exercens*

'It is characteristic of work that it first and foremost unites people. In this consists its social power: the power to build a community. In the final analysis, both those who work and those who manage the means of production or who own them must in some way be united in this community. In the light of this fundamental structure of all work – in the light of the fact that in the final analysis labour and capital are indispensable components of the process of production in any social system – it is clear that, even if it is because of their work needs that people unite to secure their rights, their union remains a constructive factor of social order and solidarity, and it is impossible to ignore it' (No. 20).

'A labour system can be right, in the sense of being in conformity with the very essence of the issue, and in the sense of being intrinsically true and also morally legitimate, if in its very basis it overcomes the opposition between labour and capital' (No. 13).

3. Property for all

*Property, that is, access to earthly goods, lies at the core of any
political order. The social question is not, in the final analysis, one
of property and, for this reason, differing concepts about the way
society should be run usually also differ about how to deal with
the issue of property, above all so far as concerns the private
ownership of the means of production. Where does Catholic social
teaching stand?*

The question of property, a fair distribution of worldly goods, is
as old as the human race. Solving it is a fundamental problem
for every form of society, and how satisfactorily it is solved determines whether people live peaceably together and have an effective
social order.

Devoting worldly goods to the community

The message contained in creation, 'Be fruitful and multiply, and fill
the earth and subdue it,' (Gen. 1:28) has always been understood in
the Christian tradition as signifying that the world's goods have been
given by God the creator of human beings and of the earth not to
individuals but to all the human community to control and to put
to good use. This distribution of assets among the community is a
natural right, because earthly goods are the indispensable basis of
existence for all.

The Pastoral Constitution of the Second Vatican Council, *Gaudium
et Spes*, says: 'God intended the earth and all that it contains for
the use of every human being and people. Thus, as all men follow
justice and unite in charity, created goods should abound for them
on a reasonable basis' (No. 69). And the encyclical developing that
teaching *Populorum Progressio* adds: 'All other rights, whatever
they may be, and also property and free exchange, are subject to
this basic law' (No. 22).

This 'basic law' of earthly possessions being given to the community has to be placed in the forefront of every discussion about property. The general welfare of all has priority over particular property rights of individuals and groups. The original purpose of earthly goods is never lost, so the right to property finds its limits in the living rights of every individual as well as of humanity in general. Any social order one-sidedly favouring a few or particular groups or for that matter practically excluding whole sections of the population from personal ownership contravenes divine law and the moral order. Given present development problems worldwide, this supreme law of property must also find application in international economic relations and in the many kinds of social conflict in countries of the Third World, as indeed the encyclical *Populorum Progressio* has indicated.

A natural or divine right to a 'positive' communion of goods or collective ownership, as espoused by communism, cannot be derived from this law. On the contrary, Catholic social teaching upholds the basic principle of a 'negative' communion of goods, meaning that no one should be excluded from earthly possessions.

Right to private property

Spreading worldly goods among the whole community is not a contradiction of the right to private property. Leo XIII says: 'However, that God the Lord has passed over to all generations of man the earth for their use and enjoyment does not exclude private ownership' (*Rerum Novarum*, No. 7). It is the duty of the state and the existing social order to regulate the distribution of property. The right to possessions is a natural right which the state cannot abolish, but it nevertheless has to see to it that the way goods are distributed and used is always reconcilable with the common good and the existential rights of the individual.

The significance of private possessions is not merely that they serve to secure the existence of individuals and their families. Possessions increase social security and confer a corresponding independence of the state and its institutions. They guarantee the individual greater room for personal creativity and development as well as for responsible action.

112

It is therefore quite indispensable to any social order that everyone should have adequate and effective access to earthly goods. This right given by nature includes access to the fruits of culture such as education, art and a better style of living. Any social order which favours a particular sector of society in the acquisition of property, and in practice excludes others, contravenes human rights and the gift of worldly goods to the whole community.

Social responsibility

Possession has both an individual and a social nature; it supports individuals and their needs and at the same time remains bound to the common good (*Quadragesimo Anno*, No. 45). Even after the distribution of the earth and its goods to individuals, these goods do not stop being at the service of the community, because they constitute the basis for the existence of the whole of humanity and of every individual. One can rightly speak in this connection of the social responsibility of possessions.

The Church has defended with great firmness the rights of property against socialist and Marxist attacks, yet at the same time it has taught that property confers social obligations. It has at no time shared the view of Roman and, in more recent times, liberal capitalistic law that the owners can do what they like with what belongs to them. Quite the contrary! Since the time of the Fathers, it has been Church doctrine that everyone can freely do with what they possess only insofar as the necessities of life are concerned; and everything over and above that, the so-called surplus, they have a social obligation to use for the whole community and those in need, under pain of grave sin.

In this connection the encyclical *Quadragesimo Anno* makes a trenchant observation in the light of continuing high unemployment. It points to the social obligation of possessions in that very high incomes – in the first instance company profits – are to be placed at the disposal of the 'creation of work and earning opportunities on the grand scale' (No. 51). This places the 'high earner' in a position of severe moral obligation and great social responsibility. In such delicate questions our free and property-owning society will at the same time have to be able to defend and justify itself. The same could be said about conditions in some Third World countries.

Solving the 'social question'

It is the declared aim of all Marxist-communist theories to solve the social question once and for all by abolishing private ownership of the means of production and doing away with the capital-owning class. As capital and labour are seen as irreconcilable opposites, the process of deproletarianization is attainable only by abolishing private possession of the means of production, so that all are equal in owning nothing at all.

For Catholic social teaching, however, the class war is not a given fact of life. True, it recognizes the existence and the fate of the proletariat as being rooted in having nothing to call their own, and for this very reason the goal of the Catholic social movement is, and has been since the last century, to create a new class of workers by having them acquire possessions and so bring them into the structures of society. Such a social programme can be described very simply as deproletarianization by the acquisition of possessions and capital. Overcoming the class struggle is not to be achieved by abolishing private property, but by working people having a fair share in economic profits and in the means of production.

'Woe to you that are rich!'

When speaking of the right to property and industrial co-ownership, it should not be forgotten that for the believing Christian this is not the final word on possessions and acquiring wealth. One cannot get away from what the scriptures say about riches or from their criticism of the rich. 'Woe to you that are rich!' says Luke's gospel. 'You have nothing to gain from the kingdom of God for you have received your consolation already here on earth' (Luke 6:24). And Matthew's gospel illustrates that point drastically: 'It is easier for a camel to go through the eye of a needle, than for a rich man to enter into the kingdom of God' (Matt. 19:24).

114

In several places the scriptures refer to having to be ready to leave behind everything – home, property, family – as a prerequisite for following Christ. On the other hand the poor, the socially under-privileged, are promised 'the kingdom of God' (Luke 6:20 et seq.).

Yet the many criticisms of the rich that Jesus made cannot be regarded as a blanket condemnation, because we know from the scriptures that among the disciples were people of means who helped Jesus and the poor with what they had. And in the early Christian Church there were frequently rich men and women who subsidised the communities with their resources and built the first Christian churches.

There yet remains the eschatological warning: 'Do not lay up for yourselves treasures on earth, where moth and rust consume, and where thieves break in and steal; but lay up for yourselves treasures in heaven ... for where your treasure is, there will your heart be also' (Matt. 6:19,21). Clearly all these biblical sources are a socio-political warning to all those in authority to the effect that maximizing material welfare does not itself achieve quality of life: man does not live by bread alone.

What the Church says

Second Vatican Council, Pastoral Constitution *Gaudium et Spes*

'God intended the earth with everything contained in it for the use of all human beings and peoples. Thus, under the guidance of justice together with charity, created goods should be in abundance for all in an equitable manner' (No. 69).

'Property and other forms of private ownership of external goods contribute to the expression of personality, and provide man with the opportunity of exercising his role in society and in the economy ... Private property and an acceptable amount of control over external goods assures the individual of a highly necessary sphere for the exercise of personal and family autonomy; they should be regarded as an extension of human freedom; lastly they stimulate the exercise of responsibility and constitute one of the conditions for civil liberty . . . But private property by its very nature has a social dimension; it has its basis in the common destination of all earthly goods' (No. 71).

4. Proletarians or economic citizens?

What is the approach of Catholic social teaching to control of the means of production? This question affects the foundations both of business life and of the economic order. Talking about changing the system generally means today reassessing the ownership and the control of the means of production. Indeed, the goal of different groups often remains to seek a basic change in our existing economic and social order either by abolishing the private ownership of industry or drastically curtailing private control. This chapter deals with the attitude that Catholic social teaching takes towards this issue.

A vital, not to say decisive, problem of every social order is the just distribution of the community's resources. The topic of 'distribution of resources' is as old as humanity itself. In our own time too, and indeed *particularly* now, a satisfactory solution of this question will (it is not too much to say) determine to a considerable extent the prosperous further development and peaceful cohesion of our society.

All the current debate about placing wealth in the hands of the workers has therefore a particular social priority. Considering that growth rates are slowing down and unemployment is rising, divisions of opinion over this question seem likely to become more strident.

Ownership of the means of production

In the long history of the Catholic social movement, the matter of creating wealth among the workers has always been of great importance, particularly workers' participation in productive wealth. From the beginning, a central socio-political goal of the Catholic

117

social movement, and the groups and associations supporting it, has been to bring nearer a solution to this question by promoting workers' participation. This aim remains.

An example of this can be seen in the goals set out on 22 May 1971 in the programme of the German Catholic employees' association (KAB), which said the following: 'The institution of the right to private ownership of the means of production is by itself no guarantee of freedom for all. It is much more a matter of creating a system of ownership that makes it possible for everyone to gain access to ownership, also of the means of production, and which then grants the right of use to all and guarantees freedom to all.'

Similar demands were made in the programme of the Kolping enterprise on 7 November 1976, which pointed out that participation in the means of production effectively promoted and extended industrial co-determination and a share-out of responsibility. The German federation of Catholic businessmen (BKU) produced in 1983 concrete and detailed proposals for participation in productive wealth by every section of the community. Following that, the then West German government took a similar initiative with the fourth Wealth Promotion Law and created a legal framework to encourage and promote employees' participation in shared ownership of private enterprises.

Deproletarianization

An examination of the history of the Catholic social movement shows that it has all along regarded building up workers' wealth, in particular through their participation in productive wealth, as a major factor in the solution of the social question, in the deproletarianization of the working class. As having nothing of one's own at all was seen as the kernel of being proletarian, the social movement set itself the goal of bringing the new workers' class into the community by the acquisition of property.

Deproletarianization and the overcoming of class discord are not to be attained by the abolition of private ownership, as Karl Marx would have it, but by workers enjoying a fair share of economic profits and in the means employed to make them. The goal of Catholic social teaching has been and remains to overcome the

118

class war not by dispossessing those who 'have', but to make sure all sections of the community 'have'.

The same applies, though under different conditions, to the Third World. According to the Marxist-Leninist doctrine, deproletarianization is to be achieved solely by abolishing the private ownership of the means of production and so eliminating or at least subjugating the capitalist class. Ultimately, that means everyone in the community will be put on the same level of non-possession, as we know all too well from socialism as seen in the twentieth century. Catholic social teaching has always utterly and completely rejected this.

In fact, the very opposite is laid down, for instance, in the 1931 encyclical *Quadragesimo Anno* when it speaks of deproletarianizing the proletariat by placing wealth in the hands of the workers (No. 61). Further, the 1961 encyclical *Mater et Magistra* describes private ownership of the means of production as a natural right and calls for the workers to be drawn forward in an orderly and proper manner into sharing possession of the firms they work for (Nos. 75 and 77).

An extension of human freedom

The Second Vatican Council's Pastoral Constitution *Gaudium et Spes* speaks as follows, *inter alia*, about the importance of private property in human life: 'Private property and an acceptable amount of control over external goods assures the individual of a highly necessary sphere for the exercise of personal and family autonomy; they should be regarded as an extension of human freedom; lastly they stimulate the exercise of responsibility and constitute one of the conditions for civil liberty' (No. 71).

According to the Pastoral Constitution, therefore, private possessions create room for responsible and creative action and can be regarded as an extension of human freedom. They guarantee social security and economic independence.

On top of that, employees' participation in productive wealth has an important socio-political effect. As the Pope puts it in *Laborem Exercens*, it must be the goal of the economic order that working people are the starting point, not the end, of the economic process. No other economic measure can achieve that as effectively as industrial and economic co-ownership. For that very reason, participation of the workers in productive wealth is one of the most important socio-political tasks for the future.

Sharpening the clash over distribution

Property is a hallmark of the liberal society and economic order. Well-planned measures to increase ownership among the workers serve to strengthen and extend a democratic society. At the same time, greater participation in productive wealth among broader sections of the community would help to reduce social divisions and tensions.

In the next few years profit margins will allow only a modest increase in real wages. On the other hand, growth in output will increasingly have to be reinvested in order to get the economy going again. Clashes over the distribution of profits may well become sharper if efforts to bridge the gap between increases in productivity and rises in pay come to naught. The gap could be bridged, however, if the workers, in return for giving up increases in real wages are given commensurately larger shares in productive wealth and in this way achieve income of a totally different quality.

Economic life has its ups and downs. That was nothing new to people in former times: the seven fat years would be followed by seven lean years. Now that people have become accustomed to steady economic expansion, it is hard to accept lean years and take on board losses in real wages. Workers' participation in productive wealth offers an acceptable way out: the workers increasingly have their share of risk capital and can at least to some extent also share the effects of the bad as well as the good.

Responsible economic citizens: from workers to shareholders

To the extent that workers are allowed to share in productive wealth their career and economic position improves in quality – they are turned from salaried employees into shareholders. They are co-owners, dependent on their pay, and so instead of being economic subjects they become economic citizens with a share of the responsibility.

It is natural enough that trade unions show little interest in this development. Having workers take a share in productive wealth introduces a change in the system that does not fit into a strictly socialist or indeed Marxist viewpoint.

Workers who emerge as the possessors of wealth resources and co-owner of business capital have in the final analysis shed their proletarian status and helped to overcome class division. They are lost to the class war because revolution can no longer improve their situation but only make it worse.

There is a very clear concept behind the efforts of Catholic social teaching to have the workers share in production capital. It is the abolition of the differences in society that still exist by progressively introducing a totally different way of running society: the worker dependent on his or her wage becomes the economic citizen as co-owner – a considerable extension of industrial co-determination. To put it another way: co-ownership is co-determination of a completely new quality.

What the Church says

Pius XI, encyclical *Quadragesimo Anno*

'We consider it more advisable, however, in the present condition of human society that, so far as is possible, the work-contract be somewhat modified by a partnership-contract, as is already being done in various ways and with no small advantage to workers and owners. Workers and other employees thus become sharers in ownership or management or participate in some fashion in the profits received' (No. 65).

John Paul II, encyclical *Laborem Exercens*

'If it is true that capital, as the whole of the means of production, is at the same time the product of the work of generations, it is equally true that capital is being unceasingly created through the work done with the help of all these means of production, and these means can be seen as a great workbench at which the present generation of workers is working day after day . . .

'In the light of the above, the many proposals put forward by experts in Catholic social teaching and by the highest Magisterium of the Church take on special significance: proposals for joint ownership of the means of work, sharing by the workers in the management and/or profits of businesses, so-called shareholding by labour, etc.' (No. 14).

5. Labour's priority over capital
Does the Pope call for a new economic order?

The relationship between capital and labour determines the nature of an economic system. Following on John Paul's 1981 encyclical Laborem Exercens *the view has been expressed in various quarters that in this encyclical on human work the Pope departed from the Church's previous standpoint and in so doing had created a gap with traditional Catholic social teaching. Has the Church revised its attitude to the way economic life is regulated?*

In his encyclical, Pope John Paul II placed at the heart of his reflections the socio-ethical precept that labour has priority over capital and the means of production. As a result, it has been frequently claimed that giving labour precedence constitutes a new orientation of Catholic social teaching in the direction of a 'worker-oriented' economic and social order, creating a breach with the tradition which was oriented towards property and therefore towards capital. It is furthermore claimed that the Pope is therefore calling for the setting up of a worker-oriented economic order; and that by so doing, as Franz Klüber has put it, he has corrected the capitalistic 'falsification' of Catholic social teaching.

The priority of labour

It is clear to all that the thesis of giving labour precedence over capital is the central theme of *Laborem Exercens*. This assumption flows naturally, according to the encyclical, from the dignity of labour as grounded, not in its objective but, in its subjective dimension (No. 6). And the unique dignity of human labour lies in the fact that the subject of labour, the maker of labour, is the human being, who becomes through work the image of God (No. 4 et seq.).

123

Technology, the means of production, capital and all the rest, are nothing more than the 'fruit of human labour', for which reason the Pope treats them all as the objective dimension of that labour. Now capital can no longer enjoy priority over labour, because it is the product of labour. Even so, technology, technical progress, the means of production and capital, even though representing the objective dimension of work, still have a tendency to take the lead over the subjective dimension, i.e., capital tries to rule the roost over labour and so harms the human person's dignity and inalienable rights. Labour's priority over capital, the primacy of human beings in the process of production, carries inside it a socio-ethical demand directed at every kind of economic system – capitalist as well as socialist-collectivist. It is the error of economics and materialism to look at human work solely in the light of material factors and either directly or indirectly to subjugate it to economic forces.

The outcome of this economic viewpoint is that the human being is treated as a kind of merchandise or just a tool, although the human being is actually the primary factor (No. 7). A further result is that labour and capital are kept apart when, by the nature of the economic process, they belong together. An economic order is socially just and morally acceptable only if from its very outset it overcomes the conflict between capital and labour and establishes the precedence of labour, i.e., it makes the human being the subject of the production process (No. 13).

A new kind of economic order?

This brings us to the question: has the Pope in *Laborem Exercens* taken leave of the traditions of Catholic social teaching? Does the encyclical enforce a total change in the system, a so-called worker-oriented economic order, as has been claimed in various quarters? A worker-oriented society would be an economic order dissolving the capitalist way of life and transferring the powers of economic decision-making in society and the workplace, either entirely or to a major extent, to workers and employees.

Taking this as a starting point, the so-called Bensberg Circle published as long ago as 1976 its memorandum *Anti-socialism by Tradition?* From the perspective of left wing Catholicism, it claimed to see an anti-socialist trend in traditional social teaching and, as a counter, called for the dissolution of the existing system. As the memorandum would have it, a 'consistent socialist economic policy, seen as a permanent anti-capitalist structural reform with the aim of making a qualitative change in the system, would have the further goal of achieving a worker-oriented solution.'

But does *Laborem Exercens* really constitute a breach with tradition? Does it, as has been claimed, put forward a new line of development for Catholic social teaching? How is the encyclical to be seen in the context of what has traditionally been taught?

No break with tradition

It cannot be the Pope's intention to 'correct' by means of *Laborem Exercens* an alleged erroneous development of Catholic social teaching or to introduce a totally new line of approach. In fact, he says his concentration on the problem of work is 'not intended to follow a different line, but rather to be in organic connection with the whole tradition of this teaching and activity' (No. 2). And this is why the pronouncements in this encyclical are to be interpreted against the background of Catholic social teaching and its continuation. Anyone believing that this is a break with tradition, or that a U-turn can be read into it, must realize that such a conclusion is not drawn from the encyclical but read into it.

Nowhere does the Pope lay any claim to having a specific concrete economic and social order in mind. On the contrary, as is already known to be the function of the Church, he expounds universally applicable principles for a socially just regulation of the world of work, and hence a pattern for economic and social relations that is valid for any kind of economic order, be it oriented towards market capitalism or socialist-collectivism. On the very basis of the Christian understanding of humanity, the Pope proclaims socio-ethical principles that can be applied to any political system.

In reality, we are dealing here with the long-standing principles of the Catholic social movement. The aim is to achieve an organization of the world of work in which the dignity and rights of the workers are secure. From the subjective character of work, we can perceive that labour enjoys priority over capital, and for this reason working people should not be subordinated to economic interests. It is the task of any political order to overcome the division between capital and labour and to combine them so that both these necessary factors can work together in the best way for the common good.

Awareness of working for oneself

The encyclical does not prescribe any one kind of concrete economic order as resulting from the fundamentals of Catholic social teaching. There are a number of ways in which to achieve what is necessary in socio-ethical terms. The goal is always the same. What it comes down to is that the human being at work must have the awareness that 'he is working for himself'; it must be certain that 'when man works, using all the means of production, he also wishes the fruit of this work to be used by himself and others, and he wishes to be able to take part in the very work process as a sharer in responsibility and creativity at the workbench to which he applies himself' (No. 15).

What this encyclical calls for can be realized in various very different ways, in an economic order based on private enterprise and capitalism as well as any other. In the 19th century, the Catholic social movement intended to achieve this same goal by setting up production co-operatives, bringing capital and labour together once again and dividing the economic fruits fairly. Everyone was to be an owner and an active participant as a free working human being bearing a share of the responsibility; but all attempts along this road came to nothing.

Because of circumstances, it was later decided to pursue another course, that of socio-political reforms operated on the body of the existing capitalist order, which would alter relationships within it in line with the ethical rules already described. Milestones along this route were:

work protection laws;
industrial co-determination;
profit-sharing;
and having shares in the business.

In this way, too, the ground rules which the Pope formulates can be realized. The social market economy, if directed towards the premises the Pope indicates, and to the extent that it does so, can indeed be described as a worker-oriented order in the sense of the encyclical *Laborem Exercens*.

What the Church says

John Paul II, encyclical *Laborem Exercens*

'The structure of the present-day situation is deeply marked by many conflicts caused by man, and the technological means produced by human work play a primary role in it . . . We must first of all recall a principle that has always been taught by the Church: the principle of the priority of labour over capital. This principle directly concerns the process of production: in this process labour is always a primary efficient cause, while capital, the whole collection of the means of production, remains a mere instrument or instrumental cause' (No. 12).

6. Is capitalism unchristian?
Catholic social teaching and criticism of capitalism

Catholic social teaching has from the very outset adopted a critical attitude to capitalism in the way it developed in the 19th century in Europe. This was already quite obvious in the Catholic social movement with the first industrial development at the start of the 19th century. However, can one therefore infer from the Church's stance that capitalism is in itself unchristian and must therefore be condemned in principle? That would have consequences for our attitude to the economic system as it is now.

The opinion is often expressed in discussions on current social and economic questions that capitalism is immoral and by its very nature unchristian. For this reason some Christian groups, particularly among the socially-critical Catholic left, dismiss our present economic and social system and call for a change. It is claimed that capitalism is immoral in itself because it is directed solely at profit, remorselessly exploits the poor and the weak, harms human dignity and turns people into slaves of machine and capital. It is furthermore held to be unchristian because in essential structure it ignores the commandment to love and so infringes Christian solidarity and brotherhood. Capitalism, it is held, is incompatible with the spirit of the gospel. Of late it has even been claimed that as the encyclical *Laborem Exercens* calls for the precedence of labour over capital it seeks the eventual abolition of capitalism.

Catholic social teaching's criticism of capitalism

Criticism of capitalism has a long tradition not only in the Catholic social movement, but also in the official social teaching of the

128

Church. Ever since the rise of the industrial society and the spread of a liberal vision of the economy, the capitalist system has been the object of attack. The Catholic Church's criticism of capitalism since the beginning of the 19th century is indistinguishable in its sharpness and thoroughness from criticism by well-known socialist and Marxist writers. The bold stand against capitalism taken by the Church over the last century, however, is an almost entirely unknown chapter of social history. Social encyclicals from Leo XIII (*Rerum Novarum* 1891) to John Paul II (*Laborem Exercens* 1981) leave nothing to be desired in their clarity and their lack of equivocation. One has only to read, for example, the encyclical *Quadragesimo Anno* of 1931, in particular sections 100 to 109. There one will find the Marxist criticism of capitalism in its entirety. It is therefore rather hard to understand why today theologians in Europe, and particularly also in Latin America, so insistently harp on the Marxist analysis of society and its criticism of capitalism in their 'liberation theology'. To do this one does not have to hark back to Marx, Engels and their fellow socialists.

What is capitalism?

To be able to say whether capitalism is unchristian, it should be asked first of all what is meant by this ambiguous concept. To start with, we have to differentiate between the capitalist mentality and the capitalist system. If we are to understand from capitalism that it reflects the mentality of liberalism in the economic field, dictated solely by concern for profits and an egoistical power struggle which rejects any ethical rules in economic relationships, then that is the very kind of capitalism which has been condemned by Church social teaching everywhere and at all times. But things look different when capitalism is understood as a specific way of organizing the economy or production.

We have to draw a further distinction between the liberal concept of the state and society and the capitalist method of production. Under capitalism, production is based firstly on private economic organization (private ownership of the means of production), secondly on an orientation towards the market economy, and thirdly on a basic division between capital and labour. To avoid frequent misunderstanding, the term market economy is often used today when it would perhaps be better to term it industrial economy. In any case, economic procedure under a market economy is not to be equated absolutely with capitalism.

The capitalist economic system: not immoral

In his encyclical *Quadragesimo Anno*, Pius XI said unequivocally in section 101 that the capitalist system is not in itself immoral. The 'wrongness' or immorality, that is, the social injustice, begins only when capital is employed solely for the benefit of economic growth, and it exploits the workers. To avoid this danger, the capitalist system must be placed in a political framework and directed towards the common good.

Pius XI said that, under certain conditions, free enterprise was justified and conferred great benefits, but that the ordering of the economy should not be left entirely to the unrestrained competition of market forces. The principle of competition should never be the sole guide for the economy (Nos. 88, 110). Even so, the liberal economic concept has forcefully, and on principle, rejected social or economic control by the state or the community.

The division of labour and capital, and the resulting paid-labour relationship – two typical characteristics of the capitalist system of production – are not in themselves immoral, and hence anti-social, so long as they do not support conditions that infringe human dignity and contribute to capitalist exploitation of the labour force (No. 64). The encyclical actually recommends that the paid-labour relationship should be brought into the social contract gradually through industrial co-determination, co-ownership, and profit-sharing (No. 65).

Ultimately, the Popes have consistently defended private enterprise in economic organization as the basis of an order that is free and worthy of human dignity. In doing so they have not just confirmed private property, but also the private ownership of the means of production as a natural and therefore human right.

The free capitalist market-oriented economic order is not in itself immoral, but that does not mean that unrestrained competition can act as the necessary regulator. That is a role that has to be imposed from the outside by an economic order committed to social and ethical principles.

A just economic order

That the principles of the free market economy are not in themselves wrong, and hence cannot be immoral, can be deduced not only from the effectiveness of the system but also from the fact that planned economies in socialist countries have felt they must absorb liberal elements into their systems in order to make them work.

Radical socialists and Marxist fundamentalists may bewail this as a capitalist lapse into sin. But for the sober-minded and unprejudiced economic specialist it is no more than another proof that one cannot 'buck the market', ignore the fundamental rules of the competition of services, private initiative and private responsibility, and that one cannot abandon them even if one is going to introduce a specific ideology by force and suppression.

Anyone who wants a free, liberal and pluralist community must, considering that liberty is the supreme goal of Western humanity, support a free economy. Such an economy and a free society are a natural pair, and the basis of a free economy must be, and remains, the free market, private initiative and responsibility, competition and the determination to conduct one's own affairs.

And yet, the market and the economy should not be left to themselves. The capitalist way of doing things is an economic instrument which has to be subordinated to social and human communal goals. The market and a free economy must be placed at the service of social policy because they are merely the instruments and not ultimately society's goal. The goal must be determined only by the socio-ethical values of the community as a whole and be shaped thereby into an economic order binding on everyone and incorporated into social legislation.

These socio-ethical values are dealt with in the encyclical *Laborem Exercens*. The most important are that the opposition between capital and labour must be overcome and that labour's precedence over capital must be made secure. It is a matter of a social and economic order that measures up to the demands of human dignity that safeguards inalienably the rights of working people and makes

131

humanity, both workers and managers, the originators of labour and the economy. The encyclical mentions the cardinal points as co-determination, co-ownership and profit-sharing.

It is safe to conclude from the above that the social market economy has, to a large extent, adopted the goals set by Catholic social teaching. It would be quite misleading to describe the social market economy as just a capitalist way of running things. It is already quite different from 19th century capitalism in that it prescribes for the economy a far-reaching and detailed social framework and makes sure that government instruments act as regulators of economic developments.

What the Church says

Pius XI, encyclical *Quadragesimo Anno*

'With all his energy Leo XIII sought to adjust this economic system according to the norms of right order; hence, it is evident that this system is not to be condemned in itself. And surely it is not of its own nature vicious. But it does violate right order when capital hires workers, that is, the non-owning working class, with a view to and under such terms that it directs business and even the whole economic system according to its own will and advantage, scorning the human dignity of the workers, the social character of human activity and social justice itself, and the common good' (No. 101).

'Just as the unity of human society cannot be founded on an opposition of classes, so also the right ordering of economic life cannot be left to a free competition of forces. For from this source, as from a poisoned spring, have originated and spread all the errors of individualist economic teaching. Destroying through forgetfulness or ignorance the social and moral character of economic life, it held that economic life must be considered and treated as altogether free from and independent of all public authority, because in the market, i.e., in the free struggle of competitors, it would have a principle of self-direction which governs it much more perfectly than would the intervention of any created intellect.

But free competition, while justified and certainly useful provided it is kept within certain limits, clearly cannot direct economic life ... Therefore, it is most necessary that economic life be again subjected to and governed by a true and effective guiding principle' (No. 88).

7. Can Marxism be baptized?

The dispute with Marxism-socialism has been a constant factor in Catholic social teaching and has determined the course of the Catholic social movement since the 19th century. There is therefore nothing new about trying to find reconciliation. The Church has spoken plainly and consistently enough, which makes it all the more surprising that in some quarters attempts have been made to make it look as if the Church's decision is still open.

The question whether Marxism can, in a sense, undergo baptism is not intended rhetorically, for nowadays one hears it often claimed that capitalism is in itself immoral and unchristian and that Christ's message is basically answered only by Marxism-socialism. It is already well-known that, for instance, priests like Fernando and Ernesto Cardenal in Nicaragua have said openly that there is no contradiction between Marxism and the gospel, and that indeed the one has made the other real. For that matter, many Christians are still fascinated by Marxism and communism, but the truth is that the matter has already been settled with a very clear denial in the encyclical *Quadragesimo Anno*. Any effort after this to seek a reconciliation or to define some path to compatibility must at least in part be attributed to the fact that the concepts of communism and socialism can by their very lack of clarity mean many things to many people.

The Popes' condemnation

As long ago as 1878 the concept of socialism was dealt with extensively by Leo XIII in his encyclical *Quod Apostolici Muneris*, which, however, did not distinguish between the many different directions inside the 19th century socialist movement and condemns in its entirety the socialist view of the authority of the state, of society and of the equality of all people without distinction. This condemnation concentrates particularly on socialist attacks on the protection of property under natural law, on religion and the Church and on the existing institutions of marriage and the family. Leo XIII's encyclical *Rerum Novarum* of 1891 similarly condemns socialism on the point of the role of the workers.

Rather more differentiating in its criticism is the 1931 encyclical *Quadragesimo Anno* of Pius XI, which notes that socialism has in the meantime undergone many changes and revisions. The extreme dimension, communism, is more sharply condemned, but it also notes that in its more moderate forms socialism has come rather closer on many points to the principles of Christian teaching – without being able to slough off the basic contradiction.

Pius XI went very thoroughly into communism and Marxism in the 1937 encyclical *Divini Redemptoris*. The overall judgment contained in this encyclical still stands the test of time after more than 50 years. The Pope describes this 'new gospel which offers bolshevistic and atheistic communism as a message of salvation and redemption for mankind' as 'a system full of errors and fallacious solutions contradicting both good sense and the Divine Revelation . . . It debases and enslaves the human personality and deprives it of its rights' (No. 14).

About communist tactics the encyclical says: 'They proceed as if they were the most determined claimants and propagandists of the world peace movement; at the same time they mount a class struggle in which rivers of blood are shed, and as they feel with justice that they do not have in them the inner guarantees of peace they resort to limitless armament' (No. 57).

Libertarian socialism

Fifty or a hundred years on from these papal condemnations, it must be granted that socialism has splintered – and not just in one or two directions. In the intervening period so many different kinds of socialist systems have come into being that socialism is now for many people just a vague rhetorical term covering any call for change in existing social and economic relationships. At the turn of the century revisionism was introduced through the leadership of Eduard Bernstein (1850-1932) and this has led to the situation where so-called libertarian socialism is grounded fully and completely in the democratic system and the central principles of the original 'articles of faith' have been discarded.

Christian socialism?

The question therefore becomes all the more urgent: cannot there be something like Christian socialism? The desire for this comes from the movement for 'religious socialism' of the previous century, which in our own time has been taken up again by, among others, the 'Christians for socialism' both in Latin America and in Europe. Considering the complexity of the problems involved, the question should really be approached differently, and because it is so topical the answer must be given by reiterating the approach, which might well be termed classical, in the encyclical *Quadragesimo Anno* of Pius XI (Nos. 113-126).

This says that inside socialism development has been such that 'on occasion, it is possible to observe a remarkable approximation of socialistic propaganda to the postulates of Christian social reform'. It adds that the moderate approach of socialism has led to the revision or complete abandonment of previous positions such as the revolutionary use of force, the class struggle and the abolition of private property, resulting in the 'blending across frontiers . . . of the demands of such a moderated socialism into the utterly justified efforts of Christian social reformers'.

It is then the encyclical itself which poses the question whether, when it comes to the class struggle and private property, socialism has so altered its stance that it has 'renounced its anti-Christian being', and can, therefore, 'without yielding any Christian principles be accorded recognition and in practice be able, so to speak, to undergo baptism'.

There follows the reply: 'Socialism . . . even after it has yielded to truth and justice on the points which we have mentioned, cannot be reconciled with the teachings of the Catholic Church because its concept of society itself is utterly foreign to Christian truth' (No. 117). And when it comes to religious or Christian socialism, the encyclical says: 'Religious socialism, Christian socialism, are contradictory terms; no-one can be at the same time a good Catholic and a true socialist' (No. 120).

This judgement could be called 'Sibylline', for it leaves a number of interpretations open. As long as socialism is true socialism it remains, once and for all, incompatible with Catholic teaching about humanity and society; and a socialism that was to all intents and purposes capable of undergoing baptism would in practice no longer be socialism. In the final analysis, the decision is up to socialism itself; it is hard for those who remain outside to make the decision, because every possible programme has been campaigning under the socialist flag.

Communism in the New Testament

In this context we can happily recall the example set by the first community in Jerusalem: 'for as many as were possessors of lands or houses sold them, and brought the proceeds of what was sold and laid it at the apostles' feet; and distribution was made to each as any had need' (Acts 4:34-35). Is this not an example that is compelling for all Christians and Christian communities? That the relationship among the community was an exemplary way of life cannot be denied, but on the other hand it is worth remembering that this 'communist' Christian social structure has remained unique. The message contained in the Acts of the Apostles cannot be taken as obligatory for all Christian communities because it is very clear that the other early Christian communities did not follow this example. In any case, in Jerusalem it was not a matter of a 'communist' or indeed Marxist socialist system: it is simply recorded that these people pooled resources on a voluntary basis. So far from being an example of a 'communist' society, it is an example of Christian brotherhood and kindness.

Liberation theology

The Christian Liberation Movement in Latin America contains groups sympathetic to Marxism. Insofar as such groups claim compatibility between the gospel and Marxism, the Popes' condemnation is still fully valid. A Christian Marxism is a contradiction in itself, an attempt to square the circle.

It is often claimed that one can deny Marxism as a socialist system and vision of the world, and yet at the same time take in something of the Marxist analysis of society and criticism of capitalism; but this is open to question. After all, can Marxist ideology and its analysis of society be regarded separately? Experience has shown that anyone toying with the Marxist analysis as a rule takes on board at least part of the ideological baggage. Too many people are still not aware of this, on the one hand because of a far too naive acquaintance with Marxist theses or on the other because of a deeply regrettable lack of awareness of the economic consequences.

What the Church says

Pius XI, encyclical *Quadragesimo Anno*

'But what if Socialism has really been so tempered and modified as to the class struggle and private ownership that there is in it no longer anything to be censured on these points? . . . We make this pronouncement: Whether considered as a doctrine, or an historical fact, or a movement, Socialism, if it remains truly Socialism, even after it has yielded to truth and justice on the points which we have mentioned, cannot be reconciled with the teachings of the Catholic Church because its concept of society itself is utterly foreign to Christian truth' (No. 117).

Paul VI, encyclical *Octogesima Adveniens*

'While through the concrete existing form of Marxism one can distinguish these various aspects and the questions they pose for the reflection and activity of Christians, it would be illusory and dangerous to reach a point of forgetting the intimate link which radically binds them together, to accept the elements of Marxist analysis without recognizing their relationship with ideology, and to enter into the practice of class struggle and its Marxist interpretations, while failing to note the kind of totalitarian and violent society to which this process leads' (No. 34).

8. Humanizing the world of work

The phrase 'humanizing the world of work' permits the entire world of social policy to be drawn together. Catholic social teaching sets itself a high ethical standard because it feels itself bound by the law of the gospel and therefore this aspect of social policy determines the whole. The subject of the human soul is of such far-reaching significance that one can say it encompasses the whole of Catholic social teaching.

To talk of humanizing the world of work means to believe in the particular dignity of the human being. Only if humans are more than highly developed animals does work require a particular human quality. Reciprocally, anyone believing in the particular dignity of the human being realizes that making the world of work more humane is an inescapable obligation. That is of particular significance for practising Christians, believing as they do in the divine origin of human life and in redemption through Jesus Christ.

The dignity of the human person

According to the Christian concept, the incomparable dignity of human beings is that they are created in God's image (Gen. 1:27). As this image (*Imago Dei*), they stand in a particular relationship to God – they are God's partner in a dialogue. Human beings are the only creatures endowed with speech, and as such they have intelligence, freedom and responsibility. We say: the human being is a person. This also means that the human being is not ruled by instinct as an animal is, but has been intended by the Creator to make choices about what to do or to let be. This freedom of decision simultaneously determines human responsibility.

The personal dignity of humankind has not been destroyed by original sin. On the contrary, the unique dignity of humanity has been guaranteed by Christ's act of redemption.

Work is part of this human dignity: it flows forth from the human person in freedom and responsibility. In *Laborem Exercens*, John Paul II says that work makes the human being the image of God. The Creator instructs man 'to till and to keep' the earth (Gen. 2:15), to have dominion over the earth and to subdue it (Gen. 1:28). These biblical pictures bring to full expression the God-given dignity of humanity and human work. Work is God's mandate. God calls on people to co-operate in creating the world and to continue the work of creation.

Work is also an expression of the human being, however. Individuals place their stamp on the work they perform. At the same time this work develops each individual's own particular capabilities and skills, the unique personality of each. It is through performing work in the most general sense that the human being becomes a person.

Living as a human being in the workplace

Because work is an 'expression of the human personality', labour should not be treated as a commodity to be subjected ruthlessly to the laws of the market-place (*Mater et Magistra* No. 18). That would turn the worker into a slave or a mere tool. Working conditions should not be dictated solely by economic constraints; on the contrary, they should be compatible with human dignity. That means that they must also create space for the development of the human personality, for free decision-making and responsibility. To sum it up in one sentence: in the workplace, too, the worker must be able to be a human being. Consequently, people are not to be used up and then written off like machines.

From this starting point, we find that there are definite, precise requirements when it comes to shift, team and assembly-line working, indeed, the organization of labour as a whole. It is essential to ensure that the demands of the workplace do not create physical, mental or social damage. Social conditions at work should be worthy of human dignity: for instance, it should be possible to have normal social communication inside and outside the workplace. All too frequently, long spells of shift work make social, sporting and cultural life hard to maintain.

141

Hobbies and leisure pursuits

It is sometimes loosely argued that economic constraints impose on the humanization of work certain definite limits that cannot be gone beyond. Today's workers have lots of opportunity – so it is claimed – for the necessary physical, mental, emotional and social relaxation outside their work, because they have so much more leisure time. However, people who say this ignore the fact that many people do not know what to do with their spare time, and the question must therefore be asked whether the problem should be looked at in a different way.

The workplace is too often thought of solely as a centre of production, but for the people employed there it is the place where the greater part of each working day is spent – so it would be better to regard the relief of stress *at work* and the improvement of actual working conditions as more important than the extension of leisure time.

Unemployment

People out of work may be said to be out of the rat race and so free of stressful situations, yet nothing is more stressful, more inhumane, than not having a job. Even though in our system essential needs for the worker and the family may be taken care of, the situation is still one not worthy of human dignity. Any social or economic order that deprives a large part of the population willing to work of an opportunity to do so because of an egoistical preservation of economic interests must be regarded as inhumane and antisocial.

Co-determination and co-ownership

In the encyclical *Mater et Magistra* it is stated: 'The need lies in human nature itself for anyone doing productive work to be also in a position to have a say in the way things are run and to achieve the development of his personality through work' (No. 82). For Catholic social teaching the demand for industrial co-determination is founded in the nature of the human being, deep in human

142

personality. The value and dignity of the human being lie in the personal freedom of each, the capacities to make decisions and to take responsibility. This co-determination is therefore a vital part of the humanization of the world of work. It is an aspect of being human in the workplace that workers should have a part in making decisions concerning their jobs and have their share of the responsibility.

The same goes for the worker's having a share in the wealth of their firms. Any economic or social order oriented towards human dignity should have in itself the momentum to demolish as far as is possible the relationships of social and economic dependency.

The best way to ensure this is to have the worker take a share in the firm's working capital, being a co-owner of the means of production. At the same time, co-determination and co-ownership overcome the opposition between labour and capital, as urged in social encyclicals ever since *Rerum Novarum* in 1891. Any labour system is socially just and humane 'if in its very basis it overcomes the opposition between labour and capital' (*Laborem Exercens*, No. 13).

Marxism: no solution

John Paul II in *Laborem Exercens* made it plain that existing problems cannot be solved simply by doing away with private ownership of the means of production (No. 14), as demanded by Marxism-socialism. As already shown by contemporary experience, that would only lead to private possession being taken over by the state or the party – which does precisely nothing for the situation of the worker. Working conditions are not improved, the pressure on workers are not made any easier at all, and they are as dependent as they ever were. And because there are no free and independent trade unions, workers are much more in the hands of the firm, the party – and the state apparatus. Hence, during the dominance of communism, the Soviet worker has had precious little opportunity 'to work for himself'.

Sunday as a social institution

Having Sunday free is a very special contribution to the humanization of work. To have one regular day free to rest from our labours and to honour God is a unique cultural legacy of the Judaeo-Christian religious experience.

Looked at from a socio-humanitarian viewpoint, the biblical institution of a weekly day of rest for every human being (and animal) must be regarded as the Magna Carta of social legislation. The introduction of a day of rest on Sundays was an epoch-making contribution to worker protection law.

This must also be seen from the human and cultural angle. Sunday lifts human vision above the horizon of everyday matters and offers people instead something of life's further dimension. As it is put in Matt. 4:4 'man shall not live by bread alone'. As the day on which we honour God, Sunday offers not only a vision of new horizons in life, it deepens our experience of life and so gives ultimate meaning to human living, working, loving and suffering.

What the Church says

John Paul II, encyclical *Laborem Exercens*

'As a person, man is therefore the subject of work. As a person he works, he performs various actions belonging to the work process; independently of their objective content, these actions must all serve to realize his humanity, to fulfil the calling to be a person that is his by reason of his very humanity' (No. 6).

'In this context it should be emphasized that, on a more general level, the whole labour process must be organized and adapted in such a way as to respect the requirements of the person and his or her forms of life, above all life in the home . . . Besides wages, various social benefits intended to ensure the life and health of workers and their families play a part here . . . Within the sphere of these principal rights, there develops a whole system of particular rights which, together with remuneration for work, determine the correct relationship between worker and employer' (No. 19).

9. Co-determination and economic democracy

That workers should have a say in the running of their firm is doubly valued in Catholic social teaching: on the one hand, it is seen as a concept quite inseparable from humanizing the world of labour; on the other, a basic decision in favour of freedom places it against the backdrop of a free social and economic order. But does this freedom perhaps not extend to every aspect of the community? Or is it fully valid only for certain people and not for others?

Where does Catholic social teaching stand when it comes to co-determination and democracy? It is clear that in general our society has consented to the introduction of co-responsibility in the workplace by law. It has now become a cornerstone of our free market economy and at the same time a landmark for the achievement of democracy in the community.

Some hold the view that as the law stands co-determination has gone as far as it can go; others say it should be extended even further. Yet others call for the extension of co-determination in the direction of a fundamental democratization of economic life. How does the Church see all this?

Litmus test of a free society

The Christian view of humanity, the very basis of Catholic social teaching, regards the inalienable value and dignity of the human being as anchored in his or her personality. Human beings are not ruled by instinct as the animals are, they are not machines, they are not driven by computers. They are destined to decide in freedom about what they want to do and to make their own decisions as to how to develop themselves. They realize themselves only in this making of their own decisions, they become themselves, grow into their personalities. Being a person is inextricably bound up with freedom, individual choice and hence also of personal responsibility.

Work is an action of self-unfolding, self-discovery. It is quite correct, therefore, that the encyclical *Octogesima Adveniens* describes the call to co-determination as an expression of human dignity and freedom. This call is founded, as far as Catholic social teaching is concerned, in the principle of personality. Industrial processing, rationalization, specialization, automation all give the human being little room for personal development or self-realization.

The worker at the bench fears that playing the part of a cog in the apparatus will reduce him or her to the role of a soulless machine. The fear is that there is no demand for personalities, but for robots which function all too precisely and without interruption. People and their work are debased to the level of something to be bought and sold, to be changed at will. But that is not the unavoidable fate of modern industrial society, or indeed of capitalism as understood by Marx. By subjecting this to critical examination we recognize at the same time a socio-political duty. Industrial co-determination and a sharing of responsibility in the workplace are, in our view, the starting-point for demolishing situations and conditions that dehumanize and alienate.

In addition, co-determination is a litmus test of our free society. A social market economy, in which the word 'social' is not to be just a decoration, cannot accept the social aspect as being simply a matter of picking up the bits of breakdowns in the area of social welfare. Anyone sincerely believing in the progress of a free economy, with its market orientation, cannot ignore the need for co-responsibility and shared decision-making at work.

A single-minded drive towards maximized profits and prosperity does not satisfy the modern worker. The restlessness among the younger generation, the disenchantment with existing society, are a protest against the heavy emphasis on money-making and consumerism. There is a new search for a more spiritual orientation and putting some sense back into life.

If we are not to leave this spiritual vacuum only to be filled by Marxist reformers, utopian world-improvers and pseudo-religious dreamers, we shall have to get away from our narrow economic fixations and devote ourselves a little more to the spiritual orientation

146

and humanization of communal and economic life. A necessary step towards this is the constructive acceptance of co-responsibility in the workplace and the economy in general.

Extending co-determination

As industrial co-determination is the litmus test for the capacity of our economic system to develop, we must not talk of limiting it, but of constructively extending it. The time has come for us to think again. Business is no longer to be regarded solely from an economic perspective, and therefore as a rational means for producing goods and services. Beyond that it is the place where working people live. Working conditions, the atmosphere at work and social relationships must all be put on the kind of basis where the working people can develop their own personal and social integrity, not leaving their humanity behind in the locker as they climb into their overalls.

Co-responsibility and shared decision-making must be seen as part of the humanization of the working world and the workplace. This humanization is not merely a medical, physiological and psychological matter. The personal and social aspects are just as important, because they lead to the humanization of work, in the sense that they make it become the place of a cohesive community of lives and interests.

This raises the question whether it is possible to extend co-determination inside the business from where it is now exercised in the boardroom to the shopfloor, that is, to where work is actually carried out. Workers will change their attitude to the jobs they do and the careers they pursue only when they feel that the decisions affecting them are not taken over their heads. And that leads to another question – whether it would be a good idea to extend co-determination by instituting works' committees where both employers and employees are represented.

Papal demands

To bridge the gap between capital and labour and do away with class divisions through co-determination and co-ownership lies at the very heart of the Catholic social movement and social teaching. The general line followed by the Papal encyclicals is to create a socially just economic order on the basis of fair co-operation between management and labour; not getting rid of capital, but extending control of it.

Given such an outlook, industrial co-determination and sharing in working capital are effective instruments for achieving this goal. Even cursory study of the social encyclicals makes it very clear that they do not just defend but most emphatically and energetically recommend them.

For instance, the Pastoral Constitution *Gaudium et Spes* of the Second Vatican Council recommends that 'the active participation of everyone in the running of the enterprise should be promoted . . . [taking] into account each person's function, whether it be one of ownership, hiring, management or labour' (No. 68). Co-determination and co-responsibility are anchored in the personal dignity of the human being. As the encyclical *Mater et Magistra* (No. 83) says, they constitute a demand for justice which in no way can ever be subordinated to considerations of economic returns and profitability, because the right to share in decision-making inherent in human nature is a natural right (No. 82).

Mater et Magistra makes the point once more that the goal is the humanization of the working world and the economic order. Any socially just industrial or economic system must create a sense of responsibility, enable active participation in the running of the enterprise and make room for the development of the personality. The need for discipline at work and effective management of commerce and industry does not mean having to make the working human being a mere subject, a dumb recipient of commands. The goal must always be that the enterprise becomes in itself a truly human community (Nos. 84, 91, 92).

No prescription on the form of co-determination

How co-determination is to look in reality, and what the relationship between management and labour is to be in terms of control, is not specified by the documents. This is quite in accordance with Catholic social teaching that it is not the role of the Church or its magisterium to make binding pronouncements on specific concrete economic matters; these lie within the decision-making capacity of those who are party to the proceedings and the experts involved (cf. *Mater et Magistra*, Nos. 84, 91).

What the Church says

John XXIII, encyclical *Mater et Magistra*

'We, no less than Our predecessors, are convinced that employees are justified in wishing to participate in the activity of the industrial concern for which they work. It is not, of course, possible to lay down hard and fast rules regarding the manner of such participation . . . Every effort must be made to ensure that the enterprise is indeed a true human community, concerned about the needs, the activities and standing of each of its members' (No. 91).

'Obviously, any firm which is concerned for the human dignity of its workers must also maintain a necessary and efficient unity of direction. But it must not treat those employees who spend their days in service with the firm as though they were mere cogs in the machinery, denying them any opportunity of expressing their wishes or bringing their experience to bear on the work in hand, and keeping them entirely passive in regard to decisions that regulate their activity' (No. 92).

Second Vatican Council, Pastoral Constitution *Gaudium et Spes*

'In economic enterprises it is persons who are joined together, that is, free and independent human beings created in the image of God. Therefore, taking account of the prerogatives of each – owners, employees, management or labour – and without doing harm to the necessary unity of management, the active sharing of all in the administration and profits of these enterprises in ways to be properly determined should be promoted' (No. 68).

10. Where do the unions stand now?
The German experience of trade unionism[1]

In a liberal system trade unions are an indispensable regulatory factor. No one in society disputes that they should fulfil their role of representing workers' interests. As the partner with management in wage negotiations and working conditions, in Germany they enjoy constitutional guarantees and in so doing are integrated in society as helping to keep it going. How do the unions face up to this role and to the way society is run today? How does the relationship between the Church and the unions stand?

The trade unions, brought into being in the second half of the 19th century, are an important part of free society in the West. They play a very real part in solving the social problems created by the development of the industrial economy and the dissolution of the old economic and social order of the 18th and 19th centuries. It is thanks to them that the workers have been able to win their social advancement and a greater share in the prosperity of the community as a whole. But where do they stand now, when they have attained these important goals? Given the new social questions posed by the 'post-industrial' society, what socio-political goals do they have now?

[1] There are parallels between German trade unions and those of other industrialized nations with regard to their development in their respective societies. They have now to ask themselves similar questions, although German unions have achieved far more than, for instance, British unions in terms of industrial co-determination. *(Editor.)*

The unions' campaign and achievement

In the 18th and 19th centuries the Industrial Revolution very nearly dissolved all existing political, social and economic structures. A new sector of society came into being, generally termed the proletariat, which was not integrated into the community. The workers lived on the very threshold of existence, and indeed below it. They were totally dependent politically, socially and economically and as a class had virtually no rights.

For this new industrial society and the new class there was no protection under the law, and what controls remained from the Middle Ages were swept away as a sign of liberalism. This concept of economic liberalism had a great effect on the working class. It was generally held that it was not for the state to play a regulatory or interventionist role in the economy: there was, after all, the gospel of the self-regulatory market mechanism and the free play of economic forces. It was a long time before it was realized that an active government role could not be dispensed with.

In Germany the first unions were set up in the second half of the 19th century as organizations to fight for, and to protect, the workers, and to see to it that they got their economic, social and, above all, political rights. They fought firmly and successfully against the employers' arbitrary management and exploitation, for fair wages and social security, for humane working conditions and the rights of working people.

On balance, the unions can look back with pride on what they have achieved. In the 100 years or so that they have existed, the unions have fought round after hard-hitting round to gain important goals of the labour movement: the extension of social security, steady pay increases, a place at the wage bargaining table that is constitutionally guaranteed, and industrial co-determination. Thanks to union organization, wages and salaries can be adjusted regularly to the economic growth rate. Within the framework of the legally protected right to bargain, and on the road towards industrial co-determination, the unions play an active part on the economic stage. It has been a long time since the unions were vehicles for conducting the class war. They play a public role in helping to regulate the economy, for instance as partners in wage negotiations and in the sphere of joint decision-making, and enjoy a high degree of shared responsibility for what society is today.

Power and demand

The unions' representation and power is today nearly omnipresent, broadly distributed, differentiated and often anonymous, and therefore not obvious to most people. Being the legally-protected partner in wage negotiations gives unions an unopposed power as the workers' representatives. The right to negotiate, taken together with industrial co-determination, places them in an unassailable position for influencing business decisions and the course of the economy as a whole.

On top of that, they are in Germany among the wealthiest property-holders and sometimes act in the most robustly capitalist way. They have enormous economic and financial clout. They own banks, insurance companies and consumer associations, control industrial enterprises and have extensive shareholdings.

They also have extensive political influence at both federal and state level. More than half of the elected representatives in the federal and Land governments come from the trade unions. The laws on staff representation also give the unions a share of the vote in many institutions of public administration and executive branches of government.

All this power enables them to lay claim to influence in other spheres. There is hardly an area of social and political life in which the unions do not speak up for those they represent. This right to representation has long since extended beyond traditional work and economic issues. Such universal claim to power must inevitably lead to conflict with the political parties, the Churches and other groups representing the interests of the public. There is talk in many places of the danger of the trade union state or indeed of the 'state within a state'.

Unions at the crossroads

Although they have long since attained quite a different status the unions often still act in the old way of class-warfare organizations. With their knowledge of their own strength and the goals they have set themselves, they are at a crossroads. It is up to them to decide whether they want to keep playing the role of purely campaigning organizations or whether, as a result of industrial co-determination and the right to wage bargaining and other rights of representation, they accept in full the extended role of public representation. The problem is becoming visible when, for instance, they stage strikes in firms where they already share management responsibility through co-determination.

They must ask themselves whether they stand fairly and squarely inside the current system or whether in the long term they are really after some other kind of society and economy. In trade union circles there is open talk of communal ownership, linked investment and governmental control.

To what extent do the unions accept the social market economy? Do they really want an economy that is based on free competition? At a 1978 federal congress in Hamburg of the Deutsche Gewerkschaftsbund (DGB, the trade union federation), Willy Brandt said that 'the real period of reformist policies still lies ahead of us.' What did he mean by that? Are the unions content to limit their role to representing the workers in industrial matters, or do they claim on top of that a general right of representation in every social and political question? This begins to touch, even if only tangentially, on political power sharing.

The Church and the unions

Relations between the Church and the unions are not altogether free of conflict, to put it mildly. That is as true now as it was in the past, when the unions' worldly attitudes in particular created serious differences. It should not be forgotten that socialist trade unions took part fiercely for years in anti-clerical propaganda and the fight against the Church and religion. In addition, the socio-political goals of trade unions oriented towards Marxism and the class war were, and are, incompatible with Catholic teaching; hence the creation of Christian unions in the 19th century.

After 1945 the setting-up of single-industry unions in West Germany normalized relations, but there are still differences, particularly in three areas:

Unions exceed their powers in matters of attitude to society;

154

Neutrality on the social and political attitudes of single-industry unions;
Right to representation in ecclesiastical institutions.

This is all an expression of the unions' claim to speak out on everything and become involved in social and theoretical questions, upon which they have no competence to pronounce – both because they are unions and because this infringes the principle of democratic division of powers. Two examples of taking sides in this way are abortion laws and conscientious objection to military service.

In any case, the single-industry trade union undermines the entire social structure if it permanently and gravely infringes the required neutrality on attitudes to politics and society. Christian trade unions were re-established in 1955, and for good reason.

Despite differences of opinion, the social and political necessity for vigorous trade unions is unequivocally supported by the Church. There was for a long time a dispute inside the Church as to whether Catholic workers should set up their own Christian or indeed Catholic unions or whether they should press their own interests in existing workers' associations. This fiercely contested issue was settled once and for all, in the unions' favour, in the 1931 encyclical *Quadragesimo Anno*.

As matters stand at present, unions are indispensable, a constituent part of our free society. If the system of a free social economy is to work at all, there must be strong unions because if there were not, the social balance would in the long run be destroyed. Leo XIII held the right of association to be a natural right (*Rerum Novarum* No. 38) and in *Laborem Exercens* John Paul II writes of the unions: 'Their task is to defend the existential interests of workers in all sectors in which their rights are concerned. The experience of history teaches that organizations of this type are an indispensable element of social life, especially in modern industrialized societies' (No. 20).

What the Church says

John Paul II, encyclical *Laborem Exercens*

'The modern unions grew up from the struggle of the workers – workers in general but especially the industrial workers – to protect their just rights vis-à-vis the entrepreneurs and the owners of the means of production. Their task is to defend the existential interests of the workers in all sectors in which their rights are concerned.

'The experience of history teaches that organizations of this type are an indispensable element of social life, especially in modern industrialized societies . . . Catholic social teaching does not hold that unions are no more than a reflection of the "class" structure of society and that they are a mouthpiece for a class struggle which inevitably governs social life . . . However, the role of the unions is not to "play politics" in the sense that the expression is commonly understood today. Unions do not have the character of political parties struggling for power; they should not be subjected to the decision of political parties or have too close links with them. In fact, in such a situation they easily lose contact with their specific role, which is to secure the just rights of workers within the framework of the common good of the whole of society; instead they become an instrument used for other purposes' (No. 20).

11. Strikes and lock-outs

Settling disputes between the employers and workers is an important part of the social and economic order. The German constitution, for instance, guarantees unions and management much autonomy in settling wage levels and regulation of economic matters of interest to both parties, so that the workers' right to strike and the employers' right to lock workers out are industrial weapons inside the law. But how does Catholic social teaching judge this morally? In particular, the moral propriety of lock-outs has been called into question emphatically not just by the unions but also by many Christians.

Strikes and lock-outs are legitimate weapons in industrial disputes, arising in their present form from the social strife and conflict between workers and bosses in the 19th century, but their legitimacy has since been confirmed by court judgments at the very highest level and, at the same time, restricted to specific areas of dispute. The truth of the matter is that with the passing of time a specific right to conduct industrial disputes has developed.

According to the Church's teaching, industrial conflicts are a 'necessary evil': evil because inside a just social order the goal is peace, but necessary because the workers have to fight for and protect their rights. To find this teaching, it is worth reading *Rerum Novarum* (No. 31) and, with particular regard to the right to strike, reading *Gaudium et Spes* (No. 68).

Ultimate resort

In *Laborem Exercens* Pope John Paul II says strikes are 'recognized by Catholic social teaching as legitimate in the proper conditions and within just limits' (No. 20), but that they remain 'an extreme means' or ultimate resort, not to be abused for political purposes.

It is important above all that the right to strike relates to promoting the community's general welfare. The ultimate yardstick is, and will remain, the common good, not the particular interests of one or other sector of society.

When it comes to lock-outs Church texts have not spoken out so far, but that does not mean – as is sometimes claimed – that lock-outs are forbidden for moral or Church reasons. As there are no pronouncements as yet, we are required to develop the relevant moral and juridical yardsticks from the overall stand of Catholic social teaching with the assistance of the social sciences.

Are lock-outs immoral?

The trade unions, or rather a large section of them, have been concerned for a long time to have lock-outs banned by law, even if necessary by a change in the constitution. Many trade unionists regard lock-outs as an arbitrary act by the employers designed to make the unions bleed to death and enable firms to dictate wages and working conditions, hence lock-outs are immoral and infringe human dignity, constituting an abuse of power and human beings' right to work.

This argument is anachronistic. Trade unionists making such allegations still live in the 19th century when workers and their unions stood virtually helpless against the overwhelming power of the entrepreneurs and a strike was the only weapon to oppose the often brutal behaviour of employers and defend workers' rights. That experience of suffering still has an effect among the unions.

Equality is the weapon

Relationships have changed fundamentally since then. We are living in a free and democratic society, committed by the constitution to a proper social order. The unions themselves are an institution recognized by the state both socially and under the law, and a very important part of this legal standing is the right to represent the workers at negotiations with the employers.

158

A wage settlement, however, cannot work without the consent of both parties. If one of the two had such a strong position that it could impose its will on the other, society as a whole would inevitably be the loser. Achieving wage levels that were socially fair and economically justifiable would be put into jeopardy and social harmony would be disrupted. Any imbalance in the relationship between unions and management would in the long or the short term have negative effects on the whole economy and the well-being of the individual citizen.

Now the unions like to see themselves as the underdog and say that the lock-out right gives employers an overwhelming advantage. In the whole history of the Federal Republic of Germany, as in other countries, there has not been a single case where the employers were able to dictate terms. Rather the opposite is true. The unions are one of the most powerful organs in the state, already perhaps *the* most powerful, and the employers' side has for a long time not been as powerful as it once was. The fact of the matter is that social and economic legislation has strengthened the position of working people and their unions while the influence of the employers has declined.

New strategy for the unions

A recent tactic in industrial disputes is for a union to protect its strike fund by concentrating strike action on key jobs, so crippling the entire firm, but the employer still has to keep paying wages as the majority of workers are not on strike. The employer then replies with a 'suspending' rather than a total lock-out – so the cost of the strike once again falls on the unions. The same applies to industrial action against key firms to paralyse an entire industry. The employers again reply with a restricted lock-out so that the cost of the action falls on the union.

Disputes and the law

The German court ruling of 10 June 1980 in Cassel said that any lock-out, even if only partial, is a legitimate weapon in industrial disputes, so confirming earlier judgments. The court, however, restricted the application of the lock-out: the tactic must be used only as a defensive measure to avoid the effects of a strike and never do more harm than the strike would have done – in other words, no overkill. The court held that a general ban on lock-outs would be incompatible with the existing principles of industrial negotiations.

That wage negotiations need not be preceded by industrial confrontation is shown by the 'peace pact' reached between the SMUV, the Swiss metal-workers' and watchmakers' association, and the employers in 1937. Since then there has been no official dispute. All wage rates are settled by negotiations even to this day, even though recently the industry has faced extraordinary pressures.

The way things are run in Germany at present, when it comes to negotiations between labour and management, is regarded by many as an incomparable example. But really it should be possible in a democratic society to question whether the system is the only correct one. It strains credibility if both sides adopt extreme positions for weeks on end, with or without strikes and lock-outs, when we know well enough beforehand at about what level the unions and employers are eventually going to settle. There are good reasons for questioning whether this way of running negotiations is not a relic of the 19th century, which ought to be replaced by something different in which neither party can hold the other by the throat.

What the Church says

John Paul II, encyclical *Laborem Exercens*

'One method used by unions in pursuing the just rights of their members is the strike or work stoppage, as a kind of ultimatum to the competent bodies, especially the employers. This method is recognized by Catholic social teaching as legitimate in the proper conditions and within just limits ... While admitting that it is a legitimate means, we must at the same time emphasize that a strike remains, in a sense, an extreme means. It must not be abused; it must not be abused especially for "political" purposes . . . Abuse of the strike weapon can lead to the paralysis of the whole of socio-economic life and this is contrary to the requirements of the common good of society, which also corresponds to the properly understood nature of work itself' (No. 20).

12. How social is the social market economy?

*Catholic social teaching and
the market economy*

*When the question is asked whether there is a kind of economic
order which satisfies the principles of Catholic social teaching,
the answer is frequently the social market economy. Such a glib
answer equating Church teaching with a definite economic system
shows ignorance of both. This chapter explains important basics of
Catholic social teaching in the economic field.*

The social market economy has been very successful, yet broad
sections of the population are not aware of its goals and the way
it works. It is rather like a constant supply of spring water. One
loves its freshness but never asks why it is there, where it comes
from and why the water stays clear. True, it is all rather modish
among self-styled experts such as certain television journalists and
editors, for whom capitalism is a handy term of opprobrium, to
denounce the social market economy as capitalistic and inhuman.
What then is the relationship between this economic system and
Catholic social teaching?

There is no Catholic economic order

The widely-held view that the social market economy has the same
significance as Catholic social teaching, or for that matter that one
is based on the other, rest on entirely false assumptions. It has
to be reaffirmed that a Catholic economic order does not exist,
and it could not. Catholic social teaching is primarily a matter of
principles. It is not an economic order that can be immediately
applied in various concrete situations. Rather, it works out general

principles and intrinsic ground rules for any kind of economic order seeking to be socially just and worthy of human dignity. How these principles and rules are to be applied will vary.

Adherence to a specific economic system such as, for instance the social market economy, is impossible. But, on the other hand, it would be quite feasible – and for that matter one of the tasks of Catholic social teaching – to analyse what goes on in the world in the light of the socio-ethical principles it stands for. This kind of critical examination will lead to the result that some economic systems will be held to be more compatible with Catholic social teaching, others less so and some perhaps not at all.

Concerning the social market economy more directly, it is possible to say that under certain aspects it does in practice meet some of the most important demands of Catholic social teaching. It could even be said that there is a certain affinity, which does not mean a critical distance is not to be kept. Even so, in recent times there has been an increase in the number of voices inside the Church calling for a basic denunciation of the social market economy and turning to a socialist-labourist system. Such voices often cite as an authority the encyclical *Laborem Exercens*.

What is the social market economy?

The concept of the social market economy as a free economic system was developed by liberal economists as a reaction to National Socialism. It regards as totally unacceptable every kind of government linked or centrally controlled economy. The concept itself derives from Müller-Armack, one of the fathers of the system. Looking at it in the perspective of what happens today, it presents itself as an alternative both to a complete free market system and to the centrally controlled economy, or to put it another way, as a third road between liberalism on the one hand and socialism on the other.

The social market economy is not a closed system. It is much more a model for the practical development of the economy and society, or a basic guidebook for economic policy with two important ingredients: making sure that the economy is run on market lines and that it meets its social obligations.

163

Its supporters regard the way it organizes trade and exchange as the best instrument for achieving both its economic and social goals. The law of the market and the principle of competition, however, should not become goals in themselves. The laws of supply and demand are not to determine the effectiveness of the economic and social order, but the social, personal and community needs of society at large should determine the economic framework. Which is to say that the social and communal order should harness the market economy to its own purposes.

In this the social market economy differs decisively from the capitalist economic order; it realizes that the free play of market forces is not sufficient to meet social and community needs, not even the economic requirements to achieve an optimal economic society. There has to be a super-imposed regulating and controlling function setting out the social and community framework for the economy.

The affinity to Catholic social teaching

It has already been established that the social market economy is not identical with a Catholic economic system, although it meets important criteria of Catholic social teaching, including a basic concept of individual freedom in line with the Christian ideal of self-determination, freedom and responsibility of the individual.

The social market economy seeks to ensure that working people as well as economic enterprises can attain the very highest degree of individual self-development creativity and entrepreneurial flair. That it succeeds only partially in this because of the enormous variety of economic and social blocking factors does not count against it but for it, because in a collectivist system such a drive towards free development could hardly begin.

On top of that, both the social market economy and Catholic teaching rely on a sober and realistic assessment of people as they are. All Marxist-socialist social systems and, for that matter, just as much the social-romantic system-changers (including some supporters of the Peace Movement and alternative societies) start off with a utopian view of humanity.

The social market economy takes full account of human frailty and inconsistency. This realistic assessment permits it to draw into the service of society and the economic order the human quest for possessions and profits, social recognition and individual achievement. It has become trendy to defame the principle of efficiency and competition as inhuman and ethically inferior, but they are neither, unless they are applied ruthlessly for self-aggrandizement at the expense of others or the general well-being.

Another point of contact with Catholic social teaching is the positive basic attitude to personal property and private enterprise. Catholic social teaching has always preferred private property to socialist-collectivist concepts. The goal was, and it remains, that capital and labour attain equality not through dispossession of capital but by bringing working people into ownership and a share in business.

There are so many points that could be pursued, but two worth mentioning are the principles of subsidiarity and the common good. The social market economy supports the idea of subsidiarity, which plays such a fundamental role in Catholic teaching. It is up to the state and public organizations to leave private economic and social initiative freedom for action. The totalitarian state is not a Christian ideal – not even the totalitarian welfare state. Furthermore, the social market economy has the point in its favour that it is clearly and unmistakeably committed to social responsibility, and because of that to the ethical relevance of economic activity. The common good is the goal to which every economic activity must relate.

Social components

From what has gone before, it is clear that a market economy deserves the prefix 'social' only to the extent to which social components are an essential part of its economic order. It cannot be denied there are many people brandishing the term 'social market economy' for whom this is simply a camouflage for opposing social reforms and necessary changes in the community, a handy excuse for abandoning social conscience.

A social market economy worthy of the name bears the prefix not as a decoration but as a social and ethical obligation. Tension between market and social needs cannot be totally avoided, but even so, a successful market can be directed towards the common good inside a firm social framework.

What the Church says

John Paul II, encyclical *Laborem Exercens*

'Therefore, while the position of "rigid" capitalism must undergo continual revision, in order to be reformed from the point of view of human rights, both human rights in the widest sense and those linked with man's work, it must be stated that, from the same point of view, these many deeply desired reforms cannot be achieved by an *a priori* elimination of private ownership of the means of production' (No. 14).

John XXIII, encyclical *Mater et Magistra*

'Private ownership of property, including that of productive goods, is a natural right which the State cannot suppress. But it naturally entails a social obligation as well. It is a right which must be exercised not only for one's own personal benefit but also for the benefit of others' (No. 19).

13. The entrepreneur in a free-enterprise society

In its official documents the Church has until now concerned itself with the entrepreneurs and their role in a free-enterprise society only peripherally and in connection with other matters. The encyclical Laborem Exercens *dealt directly with this subject for the very first time in the chapter about direct and indirect employers. Even so, a comprehensive assessment of the entrepreneur's importance is still awaited. What can be said about this subject from the overall point of view of Catholic social teaching?*

A national bogeyman

Do we need entrepreneurs, or can we do very well without them? For many this is a silly question, superfluous, even a rhetorical one, but we must not lose sight of the fact that for many people today the question is highly topical. In the past two decades or so entrepreneurs have become national bogeymen in some circles, and not just among young idealists. For left-wing critics they are the symbol of a system they regard as by nature inhuman and immoral, bearing the burden of blame for just about all the world's ills. The Red Brigade and other terrorist groups have murdered leaders of industry and banking not just for personal reasons but because they are seen as representatives of a detested economic and social system.

However, people in business are not under attack only from radical groups. The entrepreneur has a poor image in society, an image to which the media contribute, particularly sensational journalism. It also springs from the slanted reporting and comment acrimoniously pursued by ideologically biased writers, to say nothing of the feature series in illustrated journals and television programmes in which the role of the businessman is reduced to sheer caricature, often in the same breath that praise and adulation are heaped on stars of sport, film and television.

An economy without entrepreneurs?

A free and market-oriented economy is indispensable to a free and democratic society. Getting rid of free enterprise would lead inevitably to a centralized and state-controlled economic system. The independent entrepreneur is as much part of an open society as the liberty of the press and elections without interference. A *dirigiste*, state-controlled economy, on Soviet lines, is totally incompatible with freedom in social organization. Though criticism may legitimately and usefully be levelled at the behaviour of some people in business, anyone who wants a free society must also accept a free economic system, which means independent entrepreneurs. Wherever the laws of supply and demand are cast aside in favour of central planning and people in business are replaced by party functionaries, ideological flights of fancy will inevitably lead either to economic bankruptcy or a state-directed economy.

Left-wing critics of the system and ideological reformers are now urging a new kind of socialism, supposed to be basically different from what we have had so far and to be capable of achieving Karl Marx's humane ideals. Anyone who believes such a system will work this time round must ask why, despite all the many serious and concerted attempts in many places, it has never been possible to realize 'genuine' Marxist ideals in actual practice, neither in Cuba nor in Vietnam nor in China, and least of all in the countries of Eastern Europe.

The Marxist-communist ideal of immediate participation in all productive capital and executive management, with the worker as the direct owner, is a socialist utopia. It comes to grief simply because it asserts that the people it seeks to push forward will be immediately capable of making all the necessary decisions, able to take responsibility, and to be prepared to take the risks that private entrepreneurs undertake for their own firms.

The concept of political democracy can be applied directly to the modern business enterprise only in a limited way, because it cannot be competitive and remain in existence without determined leadership and a clear, quick-reacting and efficient capacity for decision-making. So-called worker-control systems function only in relatively small undertakings and are difficult to apply generally in a larger field. Experience has shown that such attempts end either in the bankruptcy courts or in an oppressive state system. A free society depends on free entrepreneurs.

Entrepreneurs and the market economy

In a free and democratic society there is no real alternative to the market economy. The workings of the market in a highly-developed industrial society cannot be replaced satisfactorily by a centrally-planned economy. There is no better mechanism than the market for linking multifarious consumer demands, rapidly changing needs, and differences in purchasing power, with the possibilities and the short- and long-term capacities of a large variety of individual producers.

Central planning is too cumbersome, production lead-times do not meet market demands and insufficient thought is given to cost or innovation. It is not particularly efficient, either.

The free market economy stands or falls with the creative power of a business class prepared to take risks. It is the entrepreneurs, the business executives, who in a free market keep the ball rolling. As if equipped with an array of delicate sensors, they react to every change in the market and every consumer demand.

It is thanks to them that the market economy enjoys its proven superiority over every other system. Accurately, as by computer, different enterprises respond with a variety of offers to the different and rapid changes in customers' wishes. The free market guarantees the best possible satisfaction of buyers' wishes. The free economy and free enterprise also ensure a proper and careful harnessing of the resources of capital and raw materials, because worldwide competition forces them to ceaseless effort to save costs and thereby capital and materials. On top of that, they guarantee as a rule the effective and cost-effective use of investment, because profits and losses do not affect other places and other people, but the entrepreneurs and their families directly; and profit expectations are a constant engine of progress because they permit firms to re-invest profits and inspire further creativeness even when constant competition does not compel it.

Is the profit motive immoral?

Stern criticism of the striving for profit and the pursuit of gain goes back to the very earliest Fathers of the Church. There is an unbroken Christian tradition of condemnation of the striving for possessions and economic profit which without any doubt has its roots in the New Testament. Justified as this criticism is, it should not be forgotten that at no time have economic effort, trading and dealing as such ever been condemned either in the scriptures or in Church teaching; rather, the condemnation concerns a certain attitude of spirit and the irresponsible handling of the good things of this world as well as social injustice in every form.

The profit motive is the engine of a complex industrial society and necessary progress. Every human effort can degenerate, and that applies to efficiency, success and profit as well. Economic life can rely only to a limited extent on altruism, communal solidarity and love between people, and any attempt to build a modern economy on these principles would be doomed to failure. The sole motor of the economy remains, therefore, the determination to be efficient and make a profit, unless one decides in favour of a planned economy, which must then be made to work through governmental compulsion.

Neither the striving after profit nor the free market as it was seen in the 19th century can in themselves guarantee the best possible economic achievement or social justice for everyone. The efforts of many must be linked together and directed towards the common good. The free market has to be placed inside a suitable legal framework and put at the service of society as a whole. As Oswald von Nell-Breuning has put it, the profit motive 'is a good engine but an inadequate rudder'. Steering the economy cannot be left solely to market forces.

The businessman's social responsibility

If we allow the entrepreneur a decisive role in making the free market economy work, that does not mean that every profitable deal or every initiative to make yet more profit has Christian blessing. On the contrary: it is precisely because the entrepreneur has such a useful role to play that he or she has a responsibility to match.

The Church has always taught that every possession involves an obligation to the general welfare, and that goes not just for property but for productive capacity as well. Pius XI made this quite clear in his encyclical *Quadragesimo Anno*, in which he demanded that big profits should be used to create new jobs. Every search for profit, be it ever so justified, is hedged in by the common good. It would be utterly immoral and irresponsible if people of business were to make their economic dispositions solely on the grounds of personal expectations of profit and loss without taking any account of the social consequences that would affect the individual worker and the community as a whole.

Business people may not have the sole responsibility for creating jobs and apprenticeships but still they do have a very large share. It would be against the spirit of the social market economy if they were to take the attitude that their job is to make profits in an economy that functions properly, but that the social consequences can be left to the government, the public and Church charities to deal with.

Hard times constitute a particular challenge to entrepreneurs. They have to show that they and the free market economy are in a position to solve present and future problems well and quickly. The right of entrepreneurs to exist is not guaranteed by the property rights enshrined in the constitution, but by their proven ability to be better at overcoming problems, and their capacity to use the advantages the free market economy confers in a way that shows responsibility towards the community. To the extent that entrepreneurs prove this to society through their daily comings and goings in business will their negative image be wiped away and they once again gain acceptance in the community.

What the Church says

Pius XII, *Speech to Italian small industrialists (20 January 1956)*

'At the top of the list of the reasons you gave for organizing this conference you mentioned "the promotion of the irreplaceable role of the private entrepreneur", a role which embodies supremely that spirit of free enterprise upon which depends the significant progress over the past 50 years, particularly in the industrial field. This topic is not relevant only at this present time, it is also in accordance with Church teaching, which sees in what has been achieved the realization of a higher and fundamental doctrine, i.e., the transcendent vocation of the human person to something higher and of his personal responsibility before God and the human community.'

John XXIII, encyclical *Mater et Magistra*

'It should be stated at the outset that in the economic order first place must be given to the personal initiative of private citizens working either as individuals or in association with each other in various ways for the furtherance of common interests' (No. 51).

PART THREE

Christ and politics, Church and state

The previously stated principle applies to the third part of this book: the conviction that the Church has no mandate for direct involvement in economic and political life. The Church's task, its mission, is to proclaim and build the kingdom of God, which means it has not received through Christ a direct political mission and should not lay claim to having done so. Nonetheless, it has to be recognized that the Church must exercise a political responsibility. The message of Jesus is *not* apolitical, because it aims very clearly at basic changes in human relationships which must have their impact on the political scene. The Church's scriptural message provides the foundation for the ethical rules and principles Christians should live by, but not ready-to-hand political prescriptions or party political programmes, where there is always the danger of confusion between the message of God's kingdom and some political system.

In economic matters the Christian is not 'prejudiced', for it is clear that the scriptures, the New Testament in particular, contain no absolutely direct guidelines for today's industrialized society. Politics, however, are a different matter: the radical pronouncements in the Sermon on the Mount and the eschatological perspectives of the proclamation of the divine kingdom put forward extreme socio-political themes and, indeed, utopian proposals for the way society should be run. We only need to think of the debates on disarmament and securing peace and a basic problem arises: how can these radical New Testament ethical ideas be translated into practical politics? Jesus' commandment about non-violence stands right at the heart of this.

And then there is an even more basic question: to what extent can God's kingdom be realized politically in our own time before the Second Coming? Asking these questions is not new: they have been put in one way or another for the two-thousand-year history of the Church. They have always been a matter of the overall Christian teaching concerning the state and the believer's political attitude. Indeed, this part of Catholic social teaching has the longest history. It goes back in fact to apostolic times, as can be seen in consideration of the supremacy of government in Rom. 13:1-7. In what follows there will be a general review of the ground rules of political ethics by posing particular questions and raising the issue of particular historical developments to help us understand present-day Church attitudes and assessments, including, specifically, the relationship between Church and state.

1. Should the Church stay silent on politics?

The gospel should not be confused with a political message, nor the Church with a political party. If questions are asked about Christian ground rules for political life within the framework of Catholic social teaching, it has to be made clear what authority the gospel gives the Church and the Christian to make political pronouncements. The danger has to be avoided of the gospel being misused for political purposes or of theology and the Church being improperly politicized. First of all, therefore, we must answer the question as to what biblical and theological authority the Church has to speak out politically.

Church and politics is, perhaps more than any other, an emotive subject. On the one side stand those who say the Church should stay out of political conflict altogether because to be mixed up in it would make for more injustice: the Church should confine itself to religious and pastoral matters and keep silent on political issues. Others criticize it for not taking a sufficiently strong line and urge a greater involvement in major decisions in national and international politics.

It is already a commonplace that any Church statement on a political issue is met with outraged reaction, violent criticism and widespread lack of understanding. All too often it emerges that the criticism has a rather thinner factual basis than at first appeared and that the critic holds biased views which he or she does not find in the statement.

As most people tend to judge political issues in terms of religious affiliation there is a vast field here both for religious activists and political fanatics. Many Christians are therefore asking whether it would be wiser if the Church were to stay out of politics as far as practicable.

Politicizing the Church?

There has always been a danger of the Church becoming politicized. Milestones in this were the conversion of the Emperor Constantine and the medieval alliance of Church and state. Political theology is neither in substance nor in concept anything new. Since the time of the ancients and the Stoic philosophers critical awareness has been sharpened by adopting religion into the world of politics as a basis for making an attitude or a course of action look legitimate: a prince adopts a certain policy and gives it legitimacy by theological justification and providing it with the halo of divine inspiration. Where theology allows itself to be taken into service by politics it achieves power and influence over the state. There are many sad illustrations in the history of the Church of the consequences of such an unholy mixture of religion and politics and the abuse of religion for political purposes.

It is therefore all the more remarkable that in our own day in so many Church circles there are repeated calls, made publicly and without serious thought, for introducing theology and Church pronouncements for clearly defined political aims. We are clearly living in an era of renaissance of political theology and the negative effects of a politicizing theology are revealed almost daily: political perversion of religious services, the abuse of Church statements for political purposes, one-sided and political interpretation of the scriptures, theological-biblical 'justification' of political action right up to the theological legitimation of the use of force to achieve political goals.

The ayatollahs

The gospel does not contain detailed political instructions. And it is rare that a political course of action or a decision for specific circumstances can be taken straight from scripture. In view of this, it is understandable that politicized Christians have the almost overwhelming temptation to justify their political point of view with highly selective references to the Bible and then damn those who disagree as holding opinions that are both unbiblical and unchristian. When one political belief is claimed to be the

176

only possible Christian point of view, all the others are placed beyond the pale: the Christianity of those who think differently is called into question and their attitudes are dismissed as treason of the gospel. This is often seen on both sides of the political spectrum, particularly in debates about defence, nuclear weapons, disarmament and the like.

The danger of the faith and the Church being politicized comes today not so much from its teachers and officials as from self-appointed ayatollahs among scientists, Christian politicians and lay people involved in the social and socio-political fields. Very often it is the Sermon on the Mount that is turned into a political programme, ecstatically adopted into the corpus of political activity. Even though it is not a matter of theological dispute that what Jesus said was not aimed at political change and that he was not a social revolutionary, certain contemporary reform movements – inspired by a fundamentalist interpretation of the Bible – never tire of taking the scriptures as the basis for political demands and concrete reform programmes.

Whenever Church representatives and office-bearers issue political statements, there is the danger of misuse of the religious office. The greatest care must be exercised in differentiating between the *theological content* of the message of Jesus and the *political involvement* of Christians in the community and government, and between the Church's *pastoral duty* to care for souls and its *political responsibility*, which cannot and should not be disputed. No one, whether sympathizer or critic, can equate or even seek to equate the Christian message with any particular political programme.

'Render unto Caesar . . . '

St Matthew reports that Jesus said: 'Render therefore to Caesar the things that are Caesar's; and to God the things that are God's' (22:21). This frequently used quotation can easily be misinter-preted if it is taken as an absolute division between the world of faith and political reality. The difference between 'God's king-dom' and 'the world' has to be very carefully discerned although they cannot in any way be divorced from one another – a problem with which Luther wrestled all his life.

Catholic social teaching recognizes the right of many cultural fields to make their own laws and rules, including politics, economics, art, science and sport, and defends them against religious and theological claims that would lead to impermissible alienation. Pius XI makes it absolutely clear in *Quadragesimo Anno* (No. 41 et seq.) that the Church has no particular powers over practical matters and that economics, the particular subject of this book, is a field of its own. Even so, economics and morals are not to be divided in such a way that economic activity is left free from moral controls.

The Second Vatican Council emphatically recognizes that earthly realities have an autonomy of their own, but that does not mean that these various aspects of the so-called worldly life are not subject to moral judgment. We have to differentiate sharply between the practicalities of, for instance, economic activity and the ethical standards of human life, which all too often does not happen.

When it comes to politics, we must make the following distinctions:

1. Politics shape social, communal and economic life. The Church cannot and should not remain silent on such fundamental questions;
2. Politics effect change by implementing decisions on principles and values concerning practical matters, taken by society via its legislators, social groups and institutions. The Church should use the utmost restraint in these cases involving judgments concerning concrete questions as to what is opportune.

Political directives

One cannot draw from the gospel any detailed political programme or directives for political action, but this is not to be interpreted as if the message of Jesus has no connection with politics. Though the Christian message indeed contains no such programmes it clearly lays down moral principles and defines the human and social values which give direction to the human objectives of any political system. It is for political wisdom to turn Jesus' ethical-political principles and definition of moral goals into practical politics.

Although the scriptures should not be seen as a kind of political lexicon in which each key word gives a ready-made solution, or as a compendium of political maxims, throughout the Christian message there is an unchanging picture of humanity and directions for the way that Christians should conduct themselves, indicating clear goals and absolute boundaries.

It cannot be forgotten, however, that politics often involve compromise. Those who go into the political field with dogmatic or religio-moral rigour are refusing to recognize the realities of life as it is lived and the limitations of political action. This must be borne in mind when considering Church political pronouncements which are not all made in the same authoritative manner. In certain cases the Church has to express its opposition unmistakeably and irrevocably, for instance when it comes to infringements of human rights, but there are also instances where it is proper to give counsel and to warn rather than to condemn or demand. As a general rule, one could state that what the Church says on political matters is counsel rather than command.

What the Church says

1971 Synod of bishops in Rome *De justitia in mundo*

'The Church has received from Christ the task to proclaim the message of the gospel, which contains the call to be converted from sin to the love of our heavenly Father and to universal brotherhood, and, therefore, to the need for justice throughout the world. Hence the Church has the right and, indeed, the duty to speak up for justice in the social, national and international field and to condemn conditions that affront the law of basic human rights or that place the eternal salvation of humanity at risk' (No. 37).

Second Vatican Council, Pastoral Constitution *Gaudium et Spes*

'The Church by reason of her role and competence is not identified with any political community nor bound by ties to any political system. It is at once the sign and the safeguard of the transcendental dimension of the human person ... But at all times and in all places the Church should have true freedom to preach the faith, to proclaim its teaching about society, to carry out its task among men without hindrance, and to pass moral judgments even in matters relating to politics, whenever the fundamental rights of man or the salvation of souls requires it' (No. 76).

Paul VI, Apostolic Letter on the Evangelization of the World Today, *Evangelii Nuntiandi*

'Evangelization will not be complete unless it constantly relates the Gospel to men's actual lives, personal and social. Accordingly, evangelization must include an explicit message, adapted to various conditions of life and constantly up-dated, concerning the rights and duties of the individual person and concerning family life, without which progress in the life of the individual is hardly possible. It must deal with community life in society, with the life of all nations, with peace, justice and progress. It must deliver a message, especially relevant and important in our age, about liberation' (No. 29).

'We must recognize the fact that many generous Christians who are pre-occupied with the burning problems of liberation are so anxious to see the church involved in liberation that they would reduce her role to temporal activity, merely. If this were to be accepted the church would be deprived of all her true significance.

'The message of liberation which she proclaims would lose its true value and could easily be influenced and distorted by ideological groups and political parties' (No. 32).

2. The Church's political responsibility

The previous chapter dealt with the biblical-theological legitimation of political pronouncements by the Church: what follows will deal with socio-political legitimation. Looking at society and the life of politics, the question can be asked how the Church justifies its claim to exercise political responsibility and the role of a socio-critical watch-dog. How this can be placed in the context of what we know to be a democratic and pluralist society?

Can this be reconciled with the local Christian community's pastoral duties? A comparison will be made with what was said in the first chapter of Part One about Church authority in economic and social questions.

When we speak of a political responsibility in the Church, we cannot lay emphasis on a spiritualization of the faith or retreat into the Church's 'rich inner life'. We ought not to lapse into mistaken attitudes, such as an introverted community centred on worship or a community completely or mainly concerned with politics. Yet there is no doubt: the Church *has* to exercise a political responsibility which is an integral part of its duty to save souls and which is based on following Christ.

The duty to the public

The gospel is no political programme, but the good news of God's kingdom, initiated in the person and work of Jesus Christ, to which the Church gives structure in this world. The message of salvation is universal, extending to every aspect of human activity. Christ's work of redemption embraces the salvation of all human life, including its secular, communal-political and socio-economic aspects. For this reason pastoral as well as political service is an indispensable part of the mission of the Church and of all believers.

God's kingdom is already present wherever in the world there is healing and helping work: hence the message to the seventy-two disciples: 'Heal the sick that are therein, and say to them, "The kingdom of God has come near to you"' (Luke 10:9). This command to give both message and service also has a political aspect.

The Church's public duty derives directly from Christ's mission: Jesus' message is both public and political. But this duty arises also from the obvious fact that we live in a pluralist society. It would no longer be pluralist if any sector of that community, such as the Church, were to be excluded from the process of moulding public opinion. Also, the democratic state must exercise strict neutrality in certain matters and has no ethical powers of its own, hence it needs the co-operation of the Church in a very particular way: where would the state and the community find their ethical standards and values, without which peaceful and prosperous communal life would not be possible, if it were not provided by the Church and other institutions that give meaning to life?

The Church's duty as watch-dog

The Church acts as a watch-dog over the state and the community because of its divine mission and in accordance with the precepts of a pluralistic society. The Second Vatican Council declares that the Church claims the right 'to preach the faith in true freedom, to promulgate her social doctrine, and to discharge her duty among men without hindrance. She also has the right to pass moral judgments, even on matters touching the political power, wherever basic personal rights or the salvation of souls make such judgments necessary' (*Gaudium et Spes*, No. 76).

It carries on the work of the Old Testament prophets by exposing and attacking social injustice, speaking up for those who are persecuted or deprived of their rights or in need, protesting against infringement of human rights and exerting pressure on behalf of Third World countries. The Church exercises this duty of watch-dog as one of its very oldest and original tasks. But this prophetic role cannot confine itself to criticism, nor should it; it has to look into the future, to recognize the 'signs of the times', be watchful for likely trends and raise issues of which the public is not yet conscious or for which no institutional aid is yet available. If the Church were to confine itself to being a social critic, as has been urged in various quarters, such as for instance by the writer J.B. Metz, it would in the long run lose community acceptance, particularly if the criticism is not accompanied by any positive suggestions. The Church would willy-nilly be reduced to the role of know-all critic and professional pessimistic bore. Jesus Christ was never that.

Option for the poor

Jesus particularly welcomed sinners, outcasts, the poor and the sick, and so it is one of the Church's special tasks in exercising its political function to act as advocate for the underprivileged and those on the fringes of society. It has always seen it as its sacred duty to speak out for those who cannot effectively speak for themselves. The Church was and remains the advocate and spokesperson for the poor and those in need.

To that extent it is right to speak of an option for the poor, but that does not mean *for* the poor as *against* the rich. That would be contrary to Jesus' own example: he associated himself with the poor and the outcasts of society but excluded no one from his promise of salvation. In the circle of disciples there were rich men and women who gave their financial support, and the twelve named as Apostles were not poor as we would understand the term now. When today among certain interest groups in our own community and in Latin America the Church's stance in defence of the poor is taken to be anti-capitalist agitation and Jesus' criticism of the rich is clumsily misinterpreted as criticism of capitalism and an apology for class warfare, this must be condemned as ideological abuse of the gospel in support of a false political theology.

We must also deny the claim, made in justification of such an approach, that every follower of Jesus is faced with a radical decision and that this 'Christian determination' must necessarily lead to partisanship only in favour of one group of society such as the poor and the underprivileged. Partisanship in the gospel sense should never be interpreted as excluding any group from

God's kingdom or as opting for any particular social system, party or ideology. Again, that is tantamount to the abuse of religion for political purposes.

The political task of the community

The role for the local community is determined by the pastoral hierarchy of the parish's duties. The Church's pastoral role involves no direct political mandate. The pastoral necessities of the parish demand of the clergy, those with various ministries and all the bodies within the local Church, that they maintain a prudent distance from parties, political movements and organizations so that political stances do not create a barrier to those of the faithful who hold opposing views. The community as such must be open to everyone, regardless of political belief. This remains true even if perhaps one party might have more affinity to the Church than another because of its public utterances or political goals. It will never be easy, however, for the community to relate closely to those people who on the basis of their political orientation find themselves diamatrically opposed to the teaching and role of the Church. On the one hand the Church must, regardless of the circumstances, proclaim the gospel clearly in the political and social field, yet on the other it should never exclude anyone from its pastoral care.

It becomes extraordinarily difficult when the community is required to take a position with regard to some particular event, as might happen with a work stoppage, a strike or a lock-out. Often its official representatives are then expected to intervene in the Church's name or to participate in some public action. Any workers directly affected naturally expect the community to feel solidarity and to express its support for them as far as lies in its power. On the other hand, however, the community's representatives have to be aware that, when it comes to management policy in a particular firm, the Church has not the necessary power of judgment to speak and derives no such competence from the gospel.

No one can simply claim that in principle the Church, or for that matter a particular parish community, has no political responsibility: but that responsibility is restricted by its religious and pastoral goals. Before all else great care must be taken to see that the community, as an association of the faithful, is not turned into a cockpit of political strife and social polarization. By the very nature of its origin and mission, it is a source of reconciliation and of a new fraternal communion with Christ. The community must therefore see, in the first place, its task as bringing opposing factions together and as being a haven for dialogue and for the readiness to negotiate. It should never be forgotten that when it comes to real political and economic issues it is possible for Christians to hold differing convictions.

What the Church says

German bishops' conference, Letter on *The Church in Today's Pluralist Society and Democratic State (1969)*

'The Church has a very particular public duty in today's pluralist society. It cannot fall back into the "pure" spiritual religiosity of an introverted worshipping community. Through the power of its mission it has the right and the duty "to proclaim the Faith in true freedom, make known its social teaching, fulfil its task among the people without hindrance and to pass moral judgment on political issues when basic rights of the human person or the salvation of the soul require it." Recognition of this derives not just from the Church's mission but also from the self-evident pluralistic nature of our society' (No. 29).

Instruction of the Sacred Congregation for the Doctrine of the Faith, *On Christian freedom and liberation, 22 March 1986*

'It is no part of the duties of the Church's pastors to interfere directly in the creation of political systems or organization of social life. This task is the vocation of the laity, who can work in this field on their own initiative with their fellow-citizens. In fulfilling this task they must be aware that the Church's goal is the extension of Christ's kingdom in which all humanity finds its salvation and that through them the World really is ruled by Christ' (No. 80).

3. Christians and authority
'There is no authority except from God'

The relationship of Christians to government and politics has undergone many a change since the first communities were founded in the territories of the Roman Empire. Christian thought has relied extensively on the biblical authority of St Paul's epistle to the Romans, which said that Christians should be obey the authorities. It should be asked whether this still applies today. Has the modern democratic state been legitimized by divine order, so that in exercising its powers it can appeal to the will of God?

Every authority comes from God

The Christian attitude to the state and governmental authority has since the days of the early Church been regulated by the socio-ethical directions of St Paul in his epistle: 'Let every person be subject to the governing authorities. For there is no authority except from God and those that exist have been instituted by God. Therefore he who resists the authorities resists what God has appointed, and those who resist shall incur judgment ... Would you have no fear of him who is in authority? Then do what is good and you will receive his approval, for he is God's servant for your good. But if you do wrong, be afraid, for he does not bear the sword in vain; he is the servant of God, to execute wrath on the wrongdoer. Therefore one must be subject, not only to avoid God's wrath but also for the sake of conscience' (Rom. 13:1-2;4-5).

This biblical directive makes it very clear that state power derives from God and that the Christian must obey. Opposition to governmental authority is tantamount to opposition to God and the divine order. As the Bible makes clear: for the Christian, obedience to governmental authority is not just a socio-political necessity so that people can live in peace and harmony together, but obedience is a conscientious duty, because it rests directly on God's express orders. The state and its institutions have their

186

commission from God and are in his service. It is up to them to reward the good and punish the bad, in other words, to safeguard law and order. For this purpose the state 'bears the sword', i.e., it is justified and in fact has the duty of maintaining public order even with the use of force (death penalty?).

In the First Epistle of Peter (2:13-17) there are very similar instructions, from which we can presume that these texts represent what the Church as it was then felt about the relationship between Christians and authority. To what extent are they still valid for us today? Can we still say that the state is a divine institution and that the government and its institutions exercise their powers at God's command?

The throne and the altar

Christian tradition generally regards the state, and its power to punish, as a force to be reckoned with in a sinful world. The Fathers of the Church held to the view that in the kingdom of God, when there shall be a new heaven and a new earth, government will no longer be necessary. In the same tradition, Luther regarded the state as a God-given instrument to keep and safeguard order, saving fallen humanity from being taken over by the forces of evil and from damnation by its powers to discipline and protect. Hence, it is the duty of the state to ward off evil in the world by force.

Deriving its strength from the 13th chapter of the Epistle to the Romans, even in the days of the Fathers of the Church there developed the teaching of the two swords, according to which God has given Christendom two powers, or swords, one spiritual and the other temporal. The spiritual one holds sway over spiritual matters and is entrusted to the Pope and the Church; the other belongs to the world and is entrusted by God to the Emperor and the princes. Both powers, Pope and Emperor, Church and state, are God-given.

The two-sword theory was the basis of legitimation or justification for the medieval relationship between Church and state, which was a symbiosis of spiritual and earthly power. The Holy Roman Empire, the Orbis Christianus, the Christian West with all its peoples and countries held together by both Church and state, are a very powerful expression of this teaching, according to which Church and state are not seen as in opposition to one another but as joint ambassadors and office-holders for God to guide the Christian world, the one with the spiritual and the other with the worldly sword.

Against this background there developed the theocratic doctrine of government: the Emperor, king or prince were appointed by God and held office by his grace and favour. As, according to biblical teaching, the prince exercises the power of government by divine authority, his person has the halo of divinity. Appointed directly by God, he has an unassailable position. The Church played its part in this by anointing kings and Emperors with holy oil.

The authority of the liberal state

The French Revolution signified the end of the theocratic notion of government. The medieval idea of Empire and the alliance of Church and state had the ground swept away from under it by the Enlightenment and secularization. The liberal, enlightened state does not regard itself as having been constituted by God's grace; it sees its legitimacy as deriving not from God but from the people. The sovereignty of the people has taken the place of rule by divine favour. All authority emanates from the people and the organs of government exercise their power in the people's name, not in God's.

Does that mean that the epistle to the Romans has lost its validity? May we not, can we not, say that there is no authority except from God and that the power of government is still under God's mandate? It is quite certain that we can no longer interpret the epistle to the Romans the way it was done in medieval times, but that does not mean that the core of this teaching – that ultimate authority comes from God – has been superseded or contradicted. Contemporary biblical exegesis takes the view that this epistle contains no political teaching, nor does it wish to lay down rules about the metaphysical nature of the state. However, the epistle gives directives, practical rules of conduct, for the way Christians should behave towards the state and governmental authorities. These authorities safeguard order and security, punish wrong-doers, reward the virtuous, and for those purposes hold sway with the sword, and so Christians should comply with their demands. To that extent, state authority has God's mandate and the Christian has to regard it as ordained by God.

Since Leo XIII, Catholic social teaching has based the state and its authority on the social nature of humanity. The human being is by nature intended to be social and to live in communities, but life in a community is impossible without some kind of leadership. The government, and for that matter any big communal organization, must be given the proper resources to exercise its authority, to direct the differing interests towards the common good and make sure that policies are pursued to achieve that goal. Because human beings are created by God as social beings, governmental authority is an expression of God's will and such authority is indispensable if life in the community is to be pursued at any practical level at all. And so, even though the conditions have changed, the statement 'There is no authority except from God' maintains its validity for the modern state (cf. *Gaudium et Spes* No. 74).

The abuse of power

The epistle to the Romans and some other writings have in general a positive attitude towards government and state power, but that is not all the scriptures have to say on this subject: there are references, too, to the abuse of power. The Old Testament tells of a number of kings and other office-holders who act badly and are punished for their misdeeds (e.g. King David). The Prophets' open criticisms of those in authority take up a considerable part of their writings.

In the New Testament, above all in the 13th chapter of Revelations, we find the state depicted as Babylon and the Beast (dragon) and so as the anti-Christ. The state no longer serves justice and the welfare of the citizens, but has become an end in itself. It places itself in the position of God, calls for public honours as divinity and persecutes the community. Here the state has become a totalitarian power: only those who wear the sign of the Beast are allowed the right to buy and sell (Rev. 13:17), i.e., only those who accept the ruling state ideology enjoy civic privileges and have the right to exist.

This brings us to the question of the right to resist. We know that the early Christian Church solved this problem by practising passive resistance. If the government acts unjustly or desires something that is unjust the Christian need not obey: 'We must obey God rather than men' (Acts 5:29). Many Christians have paid for their loyalty to Christ and his commandments with their lives.

The power of government is therefore limited by divine law and the natural moral law. This was made clear even in the epistle to the Romans. The state is seen as having neither divine attributes nor untrammelled power. Its function is clearly defined. It has the duty to maintain order. If it no longer promotes what is good and no longer combats evil, thereby infringing the natural moral law, it loses the moral legitimacy it derives from God's mandate – and that is where the Christian's duty to obey also finishes.

What the Church says

John XXIII, encyclical *Pacem in Terris*

'Human society can be neither well-ordered nor prosperous without the presence of those who, invested with legal authority, preserve its institutions and do all that is necessary to sponsor actively the interests of all its members. And they derive their authority from God for, as St Paul teaches, "there is no power but from God" ... God has created man social by nature, and a society "cannot hold together unless someone is in command to give effective direction and unity of purpose. Hence every civilized community must have a ruling authority, and this authority, no less than society itself, has its source in nature, and consequently has God for its author." But it must not be imagined that authority knows no bounds' (No. 46).

4. The Christian, citizen of two worlds

The political behaviour of Christians has an eschatological dimen-sion: the kingdom of God is not of this world. A Christian actually lives in this world according to a law that belongs to another order – God's kingdom. He or she is therefore in a way a citizen of two worlds. This duality of existence places its stamp on everything that the Christian does in the political field, and a Christian teaching about the state has to take that into account. The structures of our society, in as far as they are of human creation, bear the character of the ephemeral and the need for improvement.

Political responsibility is inextricably bound up with the message of God's kingdom and an indispensable part of Christ's mission in the world. That may well be regarded as undisputed today, but divisions arise soon enough when it comes to the actual realization of political tasks. Anyone seeking basic clarity on this cannot and should not ignore the fact that the Bible shows that the Christian is always a citizen inhabiting two different worlds at once.

In the field of politics that means that the laws of God's kingdom as proclaimed by Jesus cannot, as a matter of principle, cover the political laws of this world. Human progress and Christian salvation, humanity in the world and the eschatological fulfilment of God's kingdom, may not be seen as having no relation to one another; they are, however, two great realities which do not belong to the same system of measurement, but which belong to entirely different spheres.

Not of this world

The Church, and with it the basis of Christian existence, do not stem from this world. Jesus said: 'My kingship is not of this world'

(John 18:36), and that is more than a statement of defence; rather it is a programmatic guide for realizing the Christian's relationship to the world and its political institutions. And so the Christian is the citizen of two worlds: not *of* this world, but sent *into* this world and *for* this world. When Jesus prayed for his disciples in the hour of his departure from them, he said: 'They are not of the world, even as I am not of the world. Sanctify them in the truth; your word is truth. As you sent me into the world, so I have sent them into the world' (John 17:16-18).

The Christian's basis for action is not the law of political life but God's Word, source of ultimate truth and indispensable pointer for political matters. And yet, although they belong to a different way of life Christians cannot stand back from political responsibility. For Christians to pull out of society and retire into a religious ghetto is not permitted. The mission of Christ's disciples is very clear: go into the world and proclaim God's kingdom, and give service in and to the world. Such service cannot exclude political participation. The basis of the Christian mission must be seen as a dialectical relationship to politics: saying at the same time both Yes and No to the world. It is true that it profits a Christian nothing to gain the whole world and to lose him or herself (Luke 9:25), but even so, Christians cannot but play their part in creating the structure of socio-political life. Their ultimate hope lies in the promise of a 'new heaven and a new earth' but such looking towards God's future dominion is no alibi for refusing to take responsibility for shaping a better and juster life here and now.

The Pastoral Constitution *Gaudium et Spes* says: 'That is why, although we must be careful to distinguish earthly progress clearly from the increase of the kingdom of Christ, such progress is of vital concern to the kingdom of God insofar as it can contribute to the better ordering of human society' (No. 39). What we do in the community affects God's kingdom just as in its turn the faith must prove itself in political and social structures.

Resist not evil!

Where do those who want to take part in political life because of their sense of Christian responsibility find their guidelines for structuring social and political life? Scripture offers very few actual directives for *immediate* political use, apart from what is said about government authority in the epistle to the Romans. Hence we face the difficult task of converting Jesus' message of the kingdom of God into advice on political action. On the one hand, we should not lose sight of the originality of what Jesus said on ethical questions, but on the other, the different nature of the political world today demands a new interpretation of what he said, so that it can be turned into practical politics.

One of the greatest difficulties is the Sermon on the Mount, with its radical challenges to the followers of Jesus in the world. How can such moral teachings be incorporated? To name but a few: 'Do not resist one who is evil. But if anyone strikes you on the right cheek, turn to him the other also' ... 'Do not be anxious about your life, what you shall eat' ... 'Judge not that you be not judged' (Matt. 5:39;6:25;7:1).

Every attempt to incorporate to the letter such exhortations into a political programme have failed in the past and would again in the future. Individuals can live according to the precepts of the Sermon on the Mount in their private lives, if they have the necessary moral energy, but in public life the renunciation of any sort of force would soon lead to chaos and, as the development of many movements has shown, to a police state. It is no use speaking of non-violent resistance here, because force is force.

This is the clearest example of the fact that God's kingdom is not of this world and that Christ's disciples must live as citizens of two worlds. For Christian politicians who wish to take their responsibilities in society and politics seriously, this means in practice to turn the impossible into the possible. This cannot be done without constant compromises and, therefore, without falling below the radical demands of the ethics of the kingdom of God. The readiness to compromise, without which political action would be impossible, need not lead, however, to shady compromises that comfortably skirt biblical radicality, however tempting that might be.

Liberation theology

Liberation theology faces this dilemma. In many Third World countries the Church finds itself being called on in the most elementary way by desperate cries for help from the poor and needy, the oppressed and persecuted. Before the forms of individual and public violence in many of these countries, it is legitimate for the Church, whose mission it is to be with the suffering and the needy, to reflect together with its faithful on the gospel's redeeming power. The gospel is a liberating message directed not just at individuals but at communities. To that extent, humanity's social and political liberation and the creation of a human and just social and economic order are not merely a clear demand of the gospel, but also a way of giving structure to God's kingdom in this world.

And yet it still holds true that the kingdom of God is not of this world, and hence cannot be brought about by technical and scientific procedures, any more than by political and strategic means. There is, however, an internal connection between Christ's salvific work and the liberation of humanity from social injustice and political repression; they cannot be separated because they are both directed at human beings. The difference, however, lies in this: the salvation brought about by Jesus also involves the social dimension of human life, but a politico-social liberation campaign or social progress can never in itself bring about a 'new heaven and the new earth'.

Dangers

There are political dangers for Christians arising from the fact that they are citizens of two worlds, and that the great ideals of the kingdom of God and the achieving of justice for humanity are in fact different in kind. First of all, Christian politicians may be tempted to place the two side by side without further thought. That would lead to a double morality: restricting the standards of the gospel to the private sphere and leaving political life to its own devices. This kind of privatization of the gospel contradicts Jesus' prophetic preaching and the Church's mission to bring that message home.

It would be just as wrong simply to equate social progress and the liberation movements with the spread of God's kingdom. Sooner or later, that would inevitably lead to the Church and theology becoming politicized. Theologians and Church organizations should be wary of turning to specific analyses of the social sciences, to ideologies or to political programmes. We should learn from Church history that this leads to the danger of theology being hijacked by politics or of the gospel being used as a tool. It would be indefensible for the discredited alliance between throne and altar to be superseded by an alliance between revolution and altar.

The critical distance from worldly affairs taught by the gospel is of importance particularly when it comes to political programmes, emancipatory messages of salvation and revolutionary liberation movements. A critical distance *must* be kept so that the costly treasure of the kingdom of God, i.e., the good news of Jesus, is not debased into false political coin and squandered.

What the Church says

Second Vatican Council, Pastoral Constitution *Gaudium et Spes*

'This Council exhorts Christians, as citizens of both cities, to perform their duties faithfully in the spirit of the Gospel. It is a mistake to think that, because we have no lasting city but seek the city which is to come,[1] we are entitled to shirk our earthly responsibilities according to the vocation of each one. But it is no less mistaken to think that we may immerse ourselves in earthly activities as if these latter were utterly foreign to religion, and religion were nothing more than the fulfilment of acts of worship and the observance of a few moral obligations. One of the gravest errors of our time is the dichotomy between the faith which many people profess and the practice of their daily lives' (No. 43).

[1] cf. Heb. 13:14

German Bishops' Conference, *The Church in today's pluralistic society and the democratic state*

'Fleeing away from the world is as little use as a Christian virtue as the glorifying of a purely "worldly world" in leading a Christian to the right way of serving the world. Also one should "let there be no false opposition between professional and social activities on the one part, and religious life on the other. The Christian who neglects his temporal duties neglects his duties towards his neighbour and even God, and jeopardizes his eternal salvation" (*Gaudium et Spes*, No. 43)' (No. 12).

5. Do the scriptures provide political standards?

The scriptures constitute the ultimate guidelines for the Christian life, not just for the private but, self-evidently, for its social and political aspects as well. Yet the gospel does not contain an immediate political message and the scriptures do not give direct instructions about politics, let alone a political programme. The procedure whereby Catholic social teaching converts general biblical into political directives should therefore be made clear, and in this connection it should be recalled what was said in the first two sections of this book about the 'method' of Catholic social teaching. In particular the chapter on 'political theology' should be taken into consideration.

Where is the source of the Christian's political standards? To what extent can, and indeed should, Christian political action be guided by the injunction of holy scripture? As we have seen, there is a deep and basic cleft between the kingdom of God and the legal powers of this world, between divine and human law. The ethos of God's kingdom, as shown for instance in the Sermon on the Mount, can only be conditionally realized in political and social structures. By what should Christian politicians be guided, when from their Christian sense of responsibility they want to help shape political and communal life? Does the gospel give us reliable and adequate norms for political behaviour?

Only the scriptures?

After the second world war there was a strengthened desire to return to scripture. This sprang from the conviction that after the collapse of the political order and the clear failure of the judicial institutions to stand up to the onslaughts of fascism and National

Socialism the political system had to be re-thought from the ground upwards. For many people the only basis was the Christian system of values and the spirit of Christian faith. In Protestant circles in particular, it was held that the right of government and the political order should be based solely and exclusively on the divine law of the scriptures.

The theological groundwork for this was laid in the 1930s by the Swiss Reformed Church theologian Karl Barth. In his conflict with National Socialism he had to admit, like many others, that Luther's teaching of two kingdoms had tended to separate private Christian life from public politics so thoroughly that in practice government and politics were left to their own devices. Very many Protestants held the view that the state was an institution based on itself, living and governing according to the law of political expediency and not the gospel. As a result, people were left virtually helpless against the injustice of the National Socialist state.

The 1934 Barmer confirmation synod corrected this division between politics and the gospel and condemned the privatization of faith as well as the false assumption that politics is a law unto itself. The synod said: 'We reject this false teaching, that suggests there are spheres in our lives in which we belong not to Jesus Christ but to other masters'.

Against the background of events which had led to the Church's crippling lack of protest against the politics of the day, it was decided in 1945 on the Protestant side to try to base both state and justice solely on the scriptures and divine law. This christological legal basis was determined largely by Karl Barth's labours, in particular his placing Christian and civil communities side by side, so that the Christian community creates the inner core of socio-political life, from which the state and society then radiate in concentric circles. Barth believed that humanity can construct socio-ethical and political standards if one applies the basic facts of the kingdom of God by analogy to the life of politics. Experience soon showed, however, that such procedure is hardly secure against subjective interpretation of the Bible. For instance, Barth urged that, because of the revelatory nature of the scriptures, there should never be secret diplomacy in any form. This attempt soon met with general rejection because it had to be admitted that the laws and structures of God's kingdom could not be applied so directly to the actualities of political life if one were not to fall into the trap of an utterly rigorous biblical fundamentalism.

Biblical foundations for politics

Anyone wanting to believe that consistent observance of the guidelines offered by scripture will avoid political error and mistakes full of consequences would soon think again after reflecting on the chequered history of Christian politics. Examples are legion of political decisions seemingly justified in biblical and theological terms turning out to be disastrously wrong in practice. One has only to recall, for instance, the witch hunts, the burning of heretics, the wars of religion and the colonial conquests. There is no safeguard against mistaken interpretations of the scriptures in political life. Scripture does not contain particular guidelines for all individual political occurrences, each determined by a different combination of factors.

The absence of this kind of guideline does not mean, however, that the message of Jesus is irrelevant to politics. There are certain political imperatives contained in the Bible which are inescapable, for instance: regard for the poor and the weak in society, protecting the worker from exploitation and unjust treatment, defending the people against the arbitrary decisions of the powerful, concern for humane living conditions, protection before the law and a just social order. But the precise way of achieving these goals in the here and now lie not in the scriptures but in the creative imagination of politicians.

The message of Jesus is not to be taken as a sort of comprehensive programme, but rather as a set of pointers showing politicians the right direction. Anyone wishing to go into politics as a result of Christian commitment will find all the necessary directives and guidelines for a political involvement consistent with biblical teaching. These guidelines are, apart from those already pointed out, the Ten Commandments, the sanctity of human life and the institutions of marriage, the family, and government, all of which are based upon the will of God.

The Christian understanding of humanity

We have to remind ourselves of the essential importance of the Christian understanding of humanity for Catholic social teaching. In the previously mentioned absence of immediate biblical directives, this teaching takes on the role of a mediator. Where there are no obvious guidelines, Christian politics should be guided by the general picture of humanity and society revealed to us in the Old and New Testaments.

This has been often emphasized by Pope John Paul II. In his opening speech to the Latin American bishops' conference in Puebla, he said: 'Thanks to the Good News, the Church possesses the truth about humanity . . . This complete truth creates the foundation of the Church's social teaching; it is at the same time the basis for true liberation.' The biblical truth about the human race, i.e., the Christian picture of humanity, is for the Pope the star to steer the course of Christian liberation policy and a fair and just structuring of the social order.

No politicizing of the Church

We should not end this chapter without pointing to the danger of the gospel and the Church becoming politicized. The political word is neither the first nor the last the Church has to utter. If political action does not spring from the sacramental source of the faith, the gospel becomes a political ideology and the faith is trivialized, reduced to political or social activity.

At the same time the (official) Church must bear in mind that in the field of politics it has competence arising only from the faith, speaking out on ethical fundamentals and moral choices. The Church does not have the task in its official teaching to carry out the practical translation of moral principles into practical politics. Indeed, practical politics fall within the competence of Christian lay people and not of the official Church.

In such matters there are usually different ways of approaching problems and different ways of solving them, and reaching the right decisions is up to the politicians, not the Church. The goals are often only to be reached through political compromises.

In any case the official Church is always careful to express itself on political issues with proper reserve, so that it does not give cause for suspicion that the gospel is being used for political purposes and does not itself become politicized. The more the Church exercises its prophetic office of guardian, the greater will be its impact on public opinion.

What the Church says

Paul VI, Apostolic Letter on the Evangelization of the World Today *Evangelii Nuntiandi*

'While recognizing the connection between them, the Church never identifies human liberation with salvation in Jesus Christ. She knows, from divine revelation, from the experience of history, and from the principles of the faith that not every idea of liberation is necessarily compatible or consistent with the evangelical understanding of man, of things and of events. She knows that the achievement of liberation, the development of prosperity and progress are not of themselves sufficient to assure the coming of the kingdom of God. The Church is indeed firmly convinced that every form of temporal and political liberation contains within itself the seeds of its own frustration, and deviates from its noble purpose if it is no part of its fundamental aim to establish justice in charity, if the burning ardour and zeal which inspire it lack a spiritual foundation and are not directed towards salvation and eternal happiness in God as the ultimate goal' (No. 35).

6. The state, the result of sin? Christian pessimism?

The various competing designs for the way society should be run are all based on varying views of humanity. Political life in particular reveals clearly to what extent people's behaviour is shaped by the way they see the world. For in Catholic social teaching, what we call Christian realism is the determining factor, as it also forms the basis of the Christian's relationship with the state and with politics as they really are.

It has to be asked whether the state is part of the created order, intended by God as part of his good design, or whether it is the result of the fall. If the state belongs to the original paradisiacal order it is basically to be seen as a positive way of organizing human life. However, if it came into being only after the expulsion from paradise, it is part of the order created by sinful humanity and bears a stigma accordingly. Such a question may seem highly theoretical at first glance, but it is the decisive principle for determining the Christian's attitude towards state and government, besides saying something about the understanding of humanity that is at the root of various political notions.

The result of sin

The view that the state and its institutions are a result of the fall goes back to the Fathers of the Church. They were convinced that paradise had no need of the state and the institutions of justice because the people in it were virtuous by nature. After the fall humanity was so morally scarred that it had to be compelled by an organized system of justice and power to carry out its moral duties towards its fellow-creatures. The state is therefore an institution spanning the era between the fall and the Second Coming, which brings out the necessity for it to have the resources of coercion and force to impose its will. This view of the function of government has been present in the Church from the Middle Ages right down to our own day. Side by side with it, there is another tradition going back to Augustine which regards the state as being founded on the nature of humanity and therefore a necessary part of the equipment of creation.

Martin Luther continued the tradition of the Church Fathers. On the basis of his teaching of justification he arrived at a thoroughly pessimistic view of humanity. Unredeemed humanity in itself is incapable of doing good and so God has given it government as an emergency measure to keep order and forcibly prevent the human race from destroying itself. This approach naturally allows the state an undue emphasis on powers of coercion and the citizen undue emphasis on the duty to obey. A moral theory of government which sees obedience as the citizen's first duty can safely justify itself through the teachings of Luther; this Protestant way of thinking had a decisive influence on the development of the Prussian state with its heavy emphasis on a sense of duty.

The gloomy view of the state is not unique to Christian theology. It is found in one form or another in other philosophical and scientific expositions on the theory of government as well. For instance, Niccolò Machiavelli (1469-1527) also took a pessimistic view of humanity; for him human beings were by nature selfish, cowardly and avaricious. Only unrelenting state power, a prince exercising rigorous control, can bring human beings to order.

Thomas Hobbes (1588-1679) also saw the human being, not as a creature living peaceably in society, but as a wild animal guided only by selfishness. In nature there is perpetual internecine warfare. To prevent self-destruction, people have agreed to subject themselves to government which can put an end to chaos and make a peaceful and orderly co-existence secure only by force.

It is self-evident that all these theories about the role of the state have one thing in common: the human being is evil by nature and therefore there has to be government, and only keeping order by force will make peaceful co-existence and cultural life possible. A pessimistic view of humanity and an over-emphasis on the power function of authority remain a characteristic of such attitudes. Ultimately, this can lead only to the idealization and religious glorification of state power, and, at the same time, too little credit being given to the individual's free and responsible action.

The state of the Enlightenment

In the Age of Enlightenment, the philosophy of government sprang from a basically optimistic view of humanity. Jean-Jacques Rousseau (1712-1778) saw humanity as good by nature, which of course belies original sin. The people subordinate themselves voluntarily to an agreement with the state on communal living (*the social contract*). The sovereign, the highest authority in the state, has the role of carrying out the common will of the community for the common good (*volonté général*). The state has to remove from the community every barrier or hindrance to the free development of the human being and to the realization of that good nature with which each was originally endowed. Education has the task of removing the child from bad influences, so that it can develop freely and its propensities for good may blossom.

The optimism of the Age of Enlightenment puts too much trust in people's natural moral fibre. It cannot deny the evil that people do, but it can and does deny that that evil has its origin inside them and instead blames environmental and social influences. The government's power to coerce is not denied but considerably played down. Much is expected, even if not everything, from the human capacity to develop freely. Within limits this philosophy has held uninterrupted sway to this day.

The same kind of optimism pervades many of our current ideas about education, training, penal reform and the like. People nowadays often blame crime not on the perpetrators but on faulty social relationships (environmentalism). On the other hand, the modern liberal 'enlightened' government is not exactly encouraged to curb individual development with the kind of firmness which would have positive results: the easy-going attitude over pornography is an example. The 'enlightened' liberal society generally tends to be sceptical of institutions and derogatory about governmental authority and power.

Karl Marx and the class state

Karl Marx (1818-1883) was also in the tradition of liberalism and the Enlightenment. According to his teaching, the state is the instrument of exploitation by those who possess the means of production. The owning class has built itself up through the introduction of private property and will vanish when ownership is abolished in the final stage of communism, which in turn will mean automatic dissolution of the state maintained by force.

Marx represents the optimism of the Enlightenment and the theory of environmental influences. He, too, thinks that the human being is virtuous by nature. When society began it was a communist society, of course, and there was neither oppression nor governmental power nor alienation nor exploitation of labour because all things were held in common. Humanity's original sin consists in the introduction of private property, with which evil made its breakthrough into society: domination by the owning class, the egoistical striving for possessions and power, the exploitation of human beings. Marx held that the abolition of private ownership would restore the human race to its original and natural state, reverting automatically to a fraternal and freedom-loving community in complete solidarity: government would be superfluous.

The trouble with this kind of utopian thinking about society is that what it sets out to do cannot be achieved without revolution and resorting to violence. First of all, force would have to be used to abolish private property, and when it becomes clear that human beings are not going to live and work together in unity and that they will continue pursuing their own selfish aims, more force will have to be used to keep the system going. By and large, communist systems have been maintained by dictatorships because they are based on an unrealistic approach to the way folk think and behave. As people will not act communistically by nature they have to be coerced into it, otherwise the system would collapse of itself.

Christian realism

Catholic social teaching, as can be seen in its official documents, takes a realistic view of humanity. It takes the evil in humanity seriously (original sin), but builds on its good intentions and positive capabilities. According to this teaching, the state arises from the social nature which the Creator has given humanity as part of its equipment from the very outset.

Human beings live in communities because that is their nature, and as this cannot be done without leadership of some kind there arises a communal authority which, in whatever form it is exercised, has to answer to that nature and to the community's needs. The authority of government is the community's supreme authority, representing society as a whole, directing individual interests and group pressures to the common good, and obliged to guarantee communal peace and public safety in the common interest.

The state, according to this teaching, is treated neither as mystical nor as an instrument of the devil. It belongs fundamentally to the creative process. The need to resort to force is the result of the fall. To call this Christian realism is justified, because people are seen as they are in their positive and negative capabilities. The slogan is: as little government as possible, as much as is necessary. The state is not entitled to limit the liberty, creativity and self-responsibility of individuals and the groups they form any more than is really necessary. But where the individual fails, it has to step in with whatever force is necessary in the interests of the community. The Christian view of humanity is based on the perception that evil lies in the heart of the human condition. It is therefore not enough for the state to change communal relationships, it has at the same time to alter human awareness and behaviour.

What the Church says

German Bishops' Conference, *The Tasks and Limits of State Authority (1953)*

'The state's moral value is based on its origin and high moral purpose. The state is neither the creature of the devil, nor the result of sin, nor the highest incorporation of the divine upon earth and an absolute aim in itself (Hegel); neither is it the arbitrary product of the force of those in power, nor is the people's will its ultimate source of justification for exercising its power (Rousseau). The state belongs much more to the moral world order desired by the Creator. Just as God is the origin of the social nature of humanity, so is also the origin of the state and the power of the state.

'Pius XII said in his Christmas message of December 1942: "The very first reason and deepest foundation of the life of the individual and society is God, Creator of the original marital union, source of the family and the community of the people and of the peoples." ' (As published in the supplement to the official Church magazine of Paderborn Archdiocese, December 1953).

7. The consequences of Emperor Constantine's conversion

Relations between Christians and government underwent a fundamental transformation when the Emperor Constantine gave the Church freedom throughout the Roman Empire and his successors declared Christianity the state religion. This was not just an event in Church history but a turning point for the way Christians see the state. It put under scrutiny the legal relationship between religion and politics, Church and state, touched on the enduring topic of government in Christian teaching, and raised the basic issue of seeing all political ethics from the Christian viewpoint. This historic development, therefore, put to the Christian world the question of 'political theology'.

One faith, one Emperor

The Emperor Constantine (306-337) gave the Church freedom in the Roman Empire and eventually Christianity became the state religion. This altered fundamentally the attitude towards government and also, naturally enough, how government and its functions should be judged. At the same time this had such a stimulating effect on how the Church saw itself, its organization and the whole world of the faith that it is fair to speak not just of the Constantinian conversion but of an ecclesiastical conversion as well.

This was not the Church's doing. It was Constantine who began the process and determined its course. The first step was certainly in the Church's interests: gaining freedom and being able to develop in public without hindrance. It recovered its confiscated assets and could win adherents, build places of worship and proclaim its teaching publicly. The Emperor gave all this his emphatic support, building churches and making generous gifts. The Church must have regarded all this as an enormous victory, particularly when it received the imperial stamp of approval, the gospel triumphing over heathen religions and false gods.

But Constantine had more in mind. He was concerned with the unity of the Roman Empire and staying in power. His motto was 'One faith, one Emperor'. He saw in the young Christianity the religion of the future and wanted to combine its vigour with the future of his Empire. He did not hesitate to take sides when he saw his efforts jeopardized by theological disputes inside the Church such as the Donatist and Arian schisms. He pursued the same political aim by giving bishops progressively more powers of government.

What the Church must have seen initially as wonderful support for the gospel message was in fact a creeping domination, nothing more than an extension of the old-established habit of government taking control of religion for its own purposes. Constantine retained the imperial title of 'Pontifex Maximus', or supreme priest, directly concerned with jurisdiction over religious affairs and regarded himself in Church terms as 'bishop for external matters'.

He interfered in Church affairs wherever and whenever he deemed it necessary. This continuation of traditional state power over religion brought about increasing identification of religion with government and the expansion of policies which bound them more closely. Yet, as developments were soon to show, all these were elements alien to the gospel message and their consequences contradicted the gospel spirit and the Church's mission.

Political theology

In the ancient world the identification of Church and state, religion and politics, was common practice. Among primitive peoples and nomads there is usually no division between the tribe and its cult. The state and the cult belong together and they constitute a unifying force. The cult, whether it be the worship of gods or ancestors or totemic, is an instrument of policy used either by the tribal chieftain or by someone he has designated, such as the holy man or witch doctor. The cult is part of the apparatus of government.

This relationship between Church and state underwent no change in the ancient world until the advent of Christianity. In the Graeco-Roman era religion and politics were generally held to have a unity which everyone understood and no one questioned, even though belief in gods was already beginning to be critically scrutinized. Government power politics harnessed religion to its purposes and religion served itself through the power of the state. The priesthood took on the role of conferring legitimacy on both the state and the ruler of the day. Emperors and kings traced their origin and hence their claim to sovereignty either to descent from divinity or enthronement by divine rites. The politics of the day were planned, interpreted and legitimized by sacrifices, oracles and auspices. Not infrequently rulers – such as the Pharaohs and the later Roman Emperors – claimed divine authority for themselves.

It is during this that the concept of 'political theology' was developed to describe the legitimation of politics and the ruling power by theology and religion. One thing 'political theology' was always notably short of was critical distance from state policy-making and those in power. Indeed, it was already involved not just in supporting some policies and claims to power but damning and eliminating others. Theology politicized becomes a political tool.

Criticism of the gospel

The arrival of Christianity meant at least in principle the end of the hitherto undisputed bond of Church and state, religion and politics. Religion and theology were now some distance from government and government policy. The message of early Christianity cast a sudden clear light on nature religions, heathen ideas about the gods, and indeed the cult of the Emperors. Nature was de-deified. Its magic as the seat of divine and demonic powers was dispelled. Instead it was presented as God's creation, something good in itself and possessing its own laws and proprieties. For the first time the worldliness of the world was spelled out without justifying its ways of behaving in its own terms or cutting it loose from its origins and ultimate goal, God.

The state lost the divine attributes derived from the cult of the Emperors and its supernatural and divine claims. It had curbs placed on it; it belonged now to the transient world, even though it still had the function of imposing order and so possessed an authority given to it by God, but at the same time was answerable to the gospel message. The Emperor was no longer the ultimate authority: 'We ought to obey God rather than men' (Acts 5:29).

The Christian owes the state obedience but no more. Identification with the government in the sense of political theology is impossible as a matter of principle. The state is not the place for the Christian to be, 'for our commonwealth is in heaven' (Phil. 3:20). God's kingdom is not of this world because it has another quality, other rules. Christians live by a different law even though they must live inside the structures of the worldly state and its society as long as the world is still there. There is an interface between God's kingdom and the world, between Church and state. Christians do not withdraw from social organization, rather they acknowledge in the freedom given by the gospel that government is a necessary instrument for imposing order. The Christian's relationship to the world and government because of the demands of the gospel is a dialectical one: in this world, but not of it.

Caesaropapism

When the Roman Empire was divided, the eastern half in its capital of Constantinople (Byzantium) developed what is generally called Caesaropapism, characterized by the identity of Church and state in a particular way: the Emperor as political ruler was at the same time temporal head of the Church, putting the Church into a position of serfdom. Backed by the political teachings of Justinian, the government exercised supremacy over the Church not just in matters of administration, finance and organization, but to a great extent in questions of faith and dogma as well.

From the outside the Church was seen to enjoy the greatest esteem and had a glittering part to play in the community. Actually it was utterly dependent, and so as time went by it turned increasingly to ritual and liturgy, a major cause of the liturgical mysticism and religious asceticism in the Orthodox Church to this day. The Church of the East never succeeded in breaking away, as far as Byzantium and in latter days Moscow were concerned, from the embrace of the Eastern Emperors and the Tsars.

The Western Church, centred on Rome, underwent a different development. The Church was able to stay free of the influence of

Caesaropapism and keep its independence from temporal rule. As this part of the Empire for a long time had no outstanding leaders, the importance and influence of the Bishop of Rome grew. The Bishop of Rome felt he had to play a more powerful role in the absence of a strong government and so he assumed temporal powers as well, which eventually led to the development of the Church-state. There was a relationship of tension and co-operation between Church and state, which the theory and theology of the two-sword concept helped to support. And that led to a new chapter in political theology.

What the Church says

German Bishops' Conference, *The Church in Today's Pluralistic Society and the Democratic State*

'Serving the Church in the world does not signify a sacerdotal alienation from temporal realities. Government and economics, science and art, have their own rules without losing their relationship to the religious. The medieval intermingling of the religious and the temporal spheres was not a Christian ideal. Certain attitudes of spirit once also held by Christians due to an inadequate understanding of science's legitimate autonomy were expressly regretted by the Second Vatican Council' (No. 8).

Second Vatican Council, Pastoral Constitution *Gaudium et Spes*

'Nevertheless there are close links between the things of earth and those in man's condition which transcend the world, and the Church utilizes temporal realities as often as its mission requires it. But it never places its hopes in any privileges accorded to it by civil authority; indeed it will give up the exercise of certain legitimate rights whenever it becomes clear that their use will compromise the sincerity of its witness or whenever new circumstances call for a revised approach' (No. 76).

212

8. The Holy Roman Empire of the Middle Ages

In the Middle Ages an attempt was made to create a 'Christian state'
in which Church, society and state form a unity. A theocracy tried
to realize God's sovereignty in politics and the community in the
name of the gospel: an important period in the long history of
'political theology'. It has to be asked whether the ideal picture of
a 'Christian state' is attainable in this world and what lessons can be
drawn for Christians and their political activity from the medieval
history of the Christian West.

The so-called two-sword theory was of great significance for determining the medieval relationship between Church and state and
also for the role of government as understood then. It contains
the basis of legitimation for the Christian state in the period and
tries to define the authority of Church and government and the
relationship between them.

Bishop Ambrose of Milan, a teacher of the Church who died in
397, in order to curb the Emperor's claim to universal power, stated
that he was (only) a member of the Church and not above it. Pope
Gelasius I (492-496) was the first to speak of the 'two powers', one
papal and the other imperial. The Emperor is not the head but a
son of the Church, but both powers are from God and are united in
God. Between the time of Christ and the Second Coming temporal
and spiritual authority here on earth are fundamentally divided.
Although in principle the Church has ultimate authority over the
state, they are independent of each other but have to work together
to effect humanity's salvation.

This developed in the course of time into the classical two-sword
teaching. God has given two powers the leadership of humanity,
the temporal sword and the spiritual sword. With the latter, *gladius
spiritualis*, the Pope reigns over the Church and matters of the spirit,
and the Emperor reigns over the government and earthly affairs with

the *gladius temporalis*. Both derive their authority from God and enjoy supremacy in their own fields, but there was controversy about the relationship between them. The Roman curial interpretation, as laid down by Pope Boniface VIII in his Bull *Unam sanctam* of 1302, placed the temporal below the spiritual power. The Pope, as the successor of St Peter, has divine authority over both: the unity of the world is incorporated in him and as he has passed on to the Emperor the temporal sword, this gives expression to his supremacy.

On the Emperor's interpretation, however, both have equal authority. Imperial jurists argued that God has given the Pope the spiritual sword but has handed the other one directly (*potestas directa*) to the Emperor, which means that temporal power is independent of the Church.

Papal alliance with the Frankish kings

The medieval unity of Church and Empire, *Sacerdotium* and *Imperium*, began with the historic alliance between the Popes and the Frankish kings. In 754 Pope Stephen II anointed Pippin and his sons in St Denis and conferred on them the title of *Patricius Romanorum*. The Pope had fled across the Alps to obtain from Pippin protection and assistance against the Langobards then harassing himself and Rome.

Since the effective protection of Byzantium had come to naught, a defence alliance was formed between the Popes and the Frankish rulers. Although the Pope initially retained his independence, he gradually drifted more and more into the position of a vassal. The Church became largely subject to the power of the state throughout the Frankish realms, the king involving himself in the Church's internal affairs, confiscating Church assets and laying claim to decision-making in matters of faith. Many of the higher clergy took up government posts.

The high-water mark of this development, an event which did much to confirm the medieval concept of government as a *Sacrum Imperium* with its far-reaching unity of Church and state, was the coronation of Charlemagne by Pope Leo III in Rome on Christmas Day 800. The Emperor received the crown from the Pope's own hand and was proclaimed Augustus and Imperator by the Romans.

This sealed the alliance between the Emperor and the papacy. The Emperor gave the Pope – and the Church – protection and security, and they in turn gave him the Church's blessing and authority over Western Christendom.

The Holy Roman Empire

The alliance between the Pope and the Frankish kings, between the Roman Papacy and the Frankish Empire, now established as the Holy Roman Empire of the German Nation, embodied the concept of a state in which the supreme moral law is the Christian faith and in which the life of the individual, the state and society as a whole are all orientated in accordance with the guiding principles of the gospel. The union of Church and state, religious life and life in the community, religious and worldly culture, became almost total.

Characteristic of this union was the fact that many religious and political offices were intermingled. Officials of government carried out important religious duties, high clerical representatives performed many of the functions of state. Prince-bishops and imperial abbots holding political as well as spiritual sway over their domains became vital supports of the Empire and its rulers. Otto's Church policy meant systematic extension of the state-church system. Bishops and abbots obtained extensive imperial possessions and rights – and to that extent they became dependants of the state and were drawn away from their religious and pastoral duties. At the same time there was a further growth of the Church itself. Local princes and the nobility made generous endowments to found and maintain churches, monasteries and other religious institutions, which created not only close collaboration but also corresponding subjection of the Church to the temporal power.

This mutual intermingling of the worldly and the spiritual went so far that the state guaranteed the execution and maintenance of Church policy in matters such as the burning of witches and the persecution of heretics. Church faith and Church law applied to the state as well. In effect there was extensive unity between state and religious law. Christian faith had successfully penetrated almost every aspect of political, social and private life.

Church decline and reform

Outwardly, the picture was most imposing. The Church was a glittering presence. Principles of the Christian faith were being applied in every corner of public and private life. There was a Christian view of government in which the faith was the power that determined every standard, in which a Christian Emperor and Christian princes ruled by divine authority and with the blessing of the Church. Was it a *civitas Dei*? Had God's kingdom come on earth?

Wherever there is much light, there is also much shadow. The price that the Church had paid was high. It was more and more dependent on the princes, who determined the appointment of priests and abbots and even Popes. Many bishops and clerics were temporal princes rather than priests and guardians of souls. Spiritual life declined, the monasteries became more and more worldly. The richer and more powerful the Church became, the further it drifted away from the gospel and from its mission.

All this close intermingling of Church and state had led to an unfortunate confusion between the spiritual and the worldly, and ultimately to the misuse of religion for political purposes and the application of politics to Church affairs: theology had become politicized and politics confused with theology.

Having arrived at the zenith of a glorious history Western Christendom offered the appalling spectacle of a bitter struggle for supremacy between the Emperor and the Pope. True enough, the Church had repeatedly tried to reform and purge itself, for instance, through the Cluniac Reforms and the Franciscan movement which encouraged poverty, but on the whole it has to be admitted that from the close links between the temporal power and the Church, between throne and altar, the Church had lost as much as it had gained.

A Christian state?

Is it possible to claim that the idea of a Christian West succeeded? To what extent had the concept been realized of a unity between

216

Church and state and of religion and society? Had the goal of a Christian Empire, an *Orbis christianus*, under the leadership of the Emperor and the Pope been achieved?

There is no simple answer to this question. Certainly the achievements of Western Christianity compel admiration. After the Enlightenment and secularization, we tend more to seek out the shortcomings and denounce the failures, rather than to give the tremendous achievements in all aspects of social, economic, cultural and religious life their proper due. One has to remember the great cathedrals, those splendid memorials to medieval builders, Western culture and Christian piety, and the contribution the monasteries made to economic, cultural and scientific progress.

Yet admiration for past achievement should not blind us when we ask whether the real goal of a Christian Empire, a *Sacrum Imperium*, has been achieved. Perhaps it is better to ask whether such high aims could be realized at all. One could really say that it has been shown time and again that God's kingdom is not of this world. These high aims are really bound to fail because of the world's 'realities' and the shortcomings of humanity. God's kingdom and the world, Church and state, religion and politics, are ultimately matters that cannot all be brought together under one roof. They cannot identify with each other because of their inherent nature. This does not mean that Church and state must be completely separated, but impermissible take-overs and blurring confusions should be avoided. The gospel dressed in the robes of political power and social splendour loses its ability to be the salt of the earth and the light of the world.

What the Church says

Boniface VIII, Bull *Unam sanctam* (1302)

'We are taught by the words of the Gospel that in this Church and in its power there are two swords, to wit, a spiritual and a temporal. For when the Apostles said, "Behold, here are two swords" – that means in the Church, since the Apostles were speaking – the Lord did not reply that it was too many, but enough. And he who denies that the temporal sword is in the power of Peter, has wrongly understood the word of the Lord when He says: "Put up again thy sword into its place." Wherefore both are in the power of the Church, namely the spiritual and material swords; the one, indeed, to be wielded for the Church, the other by the Church; the former by the priest, the latter by the hand of kings and knights, but at the will and sufferance of the priest ... The spiritual power exceeds any earthly power in dignity and nobility, as spiritual things exceed temporal ones. This we can, indeed, clearly perceive with our eyes from the giving of tithes, from the benediction and sanctification, from the recognition of this power and from the exercise of government over those same things. For, the truth bearing witness, the spiritual power has to establish the earthly power, and to judge it, if it be not good.'

9. The division of Church and state

The Age of Enlightenment finally put an end to the medieval era.
The philosophy of the Enlightenment brought the medieval view of
humanity and the world crashing to the ground, reason replacing
Christian faith as the determining and unifying power in politics
and society. The Enlightenment created a new concept of the
relationship between Church and state: instead of unity, there
had to be complete separation. Government and politics were
withdrawn from the criticism and control of faith.

The alliance of Church and state, which in the Middle Ages brought
about a unique symbiosis between spiritual and secular life, was
ended by the Enlightenment and the French Revolution. A water-
shed in this development was the imperial executive decree of
1803 abolishing the prince-bishoprics and closing more than 280
monasteries and religious foundations, most of the proceeds being
confiscated by the rulers. This ended the worldly power of many
holders of major religious office and was a major step in the
separation of Church and state – an avowed aim in the Age of
Enlightenment.

The state under the Enlightenment

The philosophy of the Enlightenment utterly rejected the principle
of the state being created from above, i.e., that it derived its power
from a transcendent God, and instead saw government authority justified and given a legal basis purely on grounds of reason.
According to Rousseau's *social contract* of 1762, the state comes
about through voluntary agreement among citizens, its authority
emanating from their consent and free will. Every form of divine
right was renounced and in its place the sovereignty of the people
was declared to be the supreme power. The regimen of government
control had to justify itself to, and be answerable to, human reason

and the will of the people alone. It was up to government to give protection to individuals and their rights to freedom (freedom of conscience, religion and opinion). The state in the Age of Enlightenment had to have a monopoly of schooling and education for all citizens.

This philosophy allowed religion and practising faith merely the right to exist insofar as they could be justified by the critical power of human reason. God's existence could be recognized as the possible seat of moral awareness, but what was emphatically rejected was the revelation of a personal God who directly determined the fate of individual human beings and who became human himself to redeem humanity by his death and resurrection. There is no room for anything supernatural in Enlightenment philosophy, hence religion must be purged of everything that cannot be tested by the light of reason. For Enlightenment thinkers Jesus Christ was merely the founder of one religion among several and the Bible a kind of textbook on morality, again to be purged of everything that lacks rational explanation, such as miracles and the driving out of evil spirits. It is useful in this connection to compare the work by Samuel Reimarus, *Fragmente eines Ungenannten (Anonymous Fragments)*, published by Lessing in 1774.

The Christian Church was recognized merely as a religious association, a society with the aim of practising religion and morality based on the teachings of Jesus of Nazareth. Enlightenment criticism was directed particularly at the Catholic Church which, with its religious teachings that imposed dogmas on the individual conscience, its hierarchical structure of authority, and the nature of the Mass and the Sacraments as a kind of mystery, was regarded as even more against Enlightenment ideas than were the practices of the Protestant Church. The right to a life of contemplation in monasteries was called into question and the vow of obedience was declared immoral for being irrational. These and similar arguments provided the basis for the secularization of the monasteries.

Religious policy and the Enlightenment

What has been said above makes clear to what extent the Enlightenment's policy on religion had as its main aim the complete separation of Church and state in all spheres of public life. In line with this also in the government sphere, all religious services and symbols were removed, for instance crosses or other such symbols on public buildings and the saying of prayers in schools. God's name was erased from constitutions and the civil code. Religious influences in the community and political life came under attack: it was proposed that civil ceremonies usually involving religion, such as baptisms, weddings and funerals, should be replaced with secular ceremonies like, for instance, youth dedication. Similarly traditional Church festivals were replaced by secular celebrations: Midsummer Day, Labour Day, Father Frost.

The Enlightenment had its eye particularly on religious influence in education, hence the campaign that continues to this day for secularization of Church and confessional schools and educational institutions, and having instead compulsory education of all children in schools without any religious affiliation. This was to extend to colleges and universities, putting Church-owned universities under state control and removing theological faculties from state high schools. This last was based on the argument that there is a fundamental contradiction between faith and knowledge, between theology and science; revealed theology is not a science.

Separation of Church and state was not to be enough: the Enlightenment set its sights much higher. Church and religion should be deprived of every legal protection and autonomy that gave them equality with the state. Instead they should enjoy only the rights and privileges of any private organization or association. This was aimed particularly at religious organizations transcending national boundaries, which of course meant in particular the Roman Catholic Church. The aim was to set up national churches and to institute a governmental supervision of churches: in effect, to create state churches.

In this part of the programme, particular importance was attached to getting rid of any form of religion based on revelation, which was regarded as supernatural and so contrary to reason: also, dogmas, supernatural truths of faith and the veneration of saints should be done away with. Liberal theology and biblical criticism set out to eliminate the accounts of miracles and the like from the scriptures.

A 'limping separation'

No one now seriously advocates the re-establishment of the relationship between Church and state that obtained during the Middle Ages and even to a certain extent into modern times. The close intermingling of religion and politics, which inevitably leads to the politicizing of the Church and theology, is not a Christian ideal. It is therefore to be welcomed that the Church is now free to pursue its own objectives, which of course include its duty to the people, free from false ties with government.

We live today in a pluralistic society, and under a democratic and neutral government the separation of Church and state is basically to be supported. Even so, complete separation does not fit the bill either. There is the greatest possible variety of social, communal and cultural issues where co-operation is not just desirable but a matter of common sense.

The protection the Church can enjoy under the law is justified because of its particular importance in society: its service to the general welfare, its particular responsibility for life in the community and in politics and the significance of religion for the life of the individual and the community. All of which means that an absolute separation would not be in anyone's interest.

What the Church says

German Bishops' Conference, *The Church in Today's Pluralistic Society and the Democratic State*

'The system that exists at present, called "limping separation" by some, and by others more accurately as "a free Church in a free state", is regarded by both the state and the Church as best answering the needs of the moment. A total separation of Church and state in the negative sense of neither recognizing the other is in the interests of neither because together they can more broadly meet their obligations to people and to the community. The Council is of the opinion that Church and state can better fulfil their mission of "meeting the personal and communal needs of equal people, the better they support correct co-operation with one another" (*Gaudium et Spes*, No. 76). It would be necessary, however, to keep under constant scrutiny the relationship between state and Church in particular issues and to adapt to changing circumstances: this also applies to treaties between state and Church' (No. 33).

10. All power emanates from the people

Giving the government an appearance of legality is central to all statecraft. How does the state justify its claim to exercise power over individuals, groups and institutions? Traditional Catholic social teaching kept in mind the words of St Paul (Rom. 13:17) and regarded the state as 'ordained by God'. It saw governmental authority as based on God's will and bound by his law. On the other hand, the modern democratic state regards its authority as based on the popular will. How is a view of the state in which the ultimate arbiter for action by authority is not divine law but electoral support to be reconciled with Catholic social teaching?

We regard the given facts of modern democracy as so self-evident that we are hardly aware of the inner problem connected with the concept of the people's sovereignty. From a literal point of view, the basis of modern democracy in which all power comes from the people contrasts with the gospel message that one should obey God rather than men. What is the attitude of the Church today, and of Catholic social teaching, to democracy as the form of government generally in existence today?

Sovereignty of the people

The question of how governmental authority obtains the stamp of legitimacy is of central importance for all social life and hence for every theory of statecraft. From where does the government derive its authority and its claim to power? The way people look at this has changed much in the course of history. In earlier days, the state laid claim to theocratic, and in our own time to democratic, legitimation.

The theory of theocratic legitimation is based on a divine

delegation of governmental authority. Either the citizen is convinced that the prince or the government of the day has been put there by God and has, by the act of enthronement, been given the right to exercise power, or the ruler enjoys the required legitimacy by claiming divine descent. The kings of Israel regarded themselves as deriving their authority from divine right or appointment, as did the Christian rulers in the West. For Jewish and Christian rulers alike, theocratic legitimation signified identification of temporal power with divine law and being responsible for exercising that authority before the judgment seat of heaven.

Apart from that, there are a number of theories based on the ideology of power which justify the state by the contention that only compulsion makes peaceable and friendly co-existence among human beings possible. According to Niccolò Machiavelli (1469-1527), only the inflexible will of the prince can keep people in order, for their own benefit. Thomas Hobbes (1588-1679) held the view that people in their natural state are permanently at war with everyone and that only the power of the state can prevent them from annihilating each other.

The democratic state we have today is the product of the Enlightenment and the French Revolution, deriving its authority not from divine appointment or gift, but from the people's will and at their urging. Every form of sacerdotal or supernatural legitimation is cast aside. The authority of government has to justify itself solely at the bar of popular will and human reasoning, including scientific knowledge and human experience. Authority is exercised not at God's instance but at humanity's and the apparatus of the law acts not in God's name but in the name of the people.

The Church and the Enlightenment

The Church hesitated for a long time over accepting the idea of people's sovereignty and recognizing the legitimacy of the modern democratic state. Its scepticism was not concerned with the form of government itself, over which there is no argument: there is no form of government specifically laid down by God. The Church is neutral towards the various kinds of government as long as they do not infringe human rights or act contrary to God's will. The doubts spring from the creation of modern democracy along the lines of Enlightenment thought, by which the state legitimizes itself solely on the basis of the popular will. This includes conscious rejection of every form of dependence of government and authority on God or supernatural moral law. The French Revolution set out to sweep away existing authority and with that the authority of religion and the Church. The sovereignty of the people means in Enlightenment terms toppling religion from its throne and putting reason in its place. Divine rule should be replaced by the rule of reason.

Beyond that, the Enlightenment actively opposed every influence of religion on public life. It rejected the supernatural origin of the Christian faith and its truths and questioned the very basis of existence of the Church and Christian belief. It declared war on religion in the form of a supernatural revelation. The idea of people's sovereignty was combined with disavowal of the supernatural authority for faith and so the Enlightenment campaigned with all its might against the Church's claim to authority. It is no wonder that the Church fought back vehemently.

These, then, are the reasons why the Roman Catholic Church, and for that matter the Protestants as well, regarded the democratic movement of the 18th and 19th centuries with the utmost scepticism. The concept of people's sovereignty as proclaimed by the Enlightenment was utterly rejected. The Church began to turn towards the democratic state very slowly.

The Church and human rights

As the Declaration of Human Rights in 1789 and 1793 arose from the spirit of the Enlightenment with its liberalism and anti-clericalism, the Church lacked for many years any positive attitude to the then proclaimed ideal of freedom, progress and emancipation. The French Revolution put forward an ideal which based human rights on autonomous reason and not on God's authority and on nature as God created it. It was understood as the liberation of humanity from alien authority, including the authority of a revealed God and in particular from the dogmatic and ethical claims of the Church. For this reason the Church felt that it had to reject the vaunted claims to freedom in general, and indeed in particular cases also to condemn them.

The first and still rather wary approach came during the pontificate of Leo XIII, who in his 1891 encyclical *Rerum Novarum* spoke up for workers' rights in regard to property, marriage and family, a fair wage, freedom of association, and humane working conditions. This was taken further by Pius XI.

The real change came with the end of the Second World War. Taking into account the fearsome injury inflicted on fundamental human rights, there developed under Pius XII a more positive approach and a gradual acceptance of human rights in general; but the Magna Carta of Catholic statements on this subject was John XXIII's 1963 encyclical *Pacem in Terris*. Beside the U.N.'s Universal Declaration of Human Rights, the Pope put an equivalent list of rights which he based on the innate value of the human being granted by God. The Second Vatican Council concluded this development with its 1965 Pastoral Constitution on the Church in today's world (*Gaudium et Spes*) and, in the same year, its declaration on religious freedom. These documents finally put an end to past misunderstandings and cleared the way for active Church co-operation with worldwide efforts for recognition and protection of human rights. This removed the last obstacles to the Church's adopting a positive attitude to modern democracy.

An affirmation of modern democracy

Western democracies today generally see themselves as looking at the world without taking sides, and the insulting attitude towards religion and the Church has been dropped. They base their rights to act freely and as sovereign institutions on the dignity of the individual, an approach that leaves the way open for further and much more penetrating metaphysical and theological legitimation. There is nothing to stop the Christian now regarding the rights of the human being as based on the dignity given by God who created humanity in his own image. A number of constitutional proclamations, including in broad terms the 1776 American Declaration of Independence, confirm this connection.

The way the Second Vatican Council opened the Church to the modern world also decisively altered the relationship with modern democracy. The Church regards itself as the People of

God, pursuing its own historical way together with all humankind and the society in which it finds itself for the time being (*Gaudium et Spes*, Nos. 3,40). Hence the Church offers society its assistance, together with everyone of good will, in promoting progress and the establishment of a just social order.

That is possible, because the Church has accepted today's pluralistic society, in which people of the most varied religious and social outlooks live together. This means general religious toleration and no more claims to absolutism, and the Church has made it clear that it is prepared to play its part in this kind of society. On that basis it is also possible for it to affirm modern democracy. The Council regards freedom in a democratic order as a moral duty for Christians and calls on everyone to take an active part in shaping such a society (*Gaudium et Spes*, No. 75).

What the Church says

Second Vatican Council, Pastoral Constitution *Gaudium et Spes*

'It is fully consonant with human nature that there should be political-juridical structures providing all citizens without any distinction with ever improving and effective opportunities to play an active part in the establishment of the juridical foundations of the political community, in the administration of public affairs, in determining the aims and the terms of reference of public bodies, and in the election of political leaders.

'Every citizen ought to be mindful of his right and duty to promote the common good by using his vote. The Church praises and esteems those who devote themselves to the public good for the service of men and take upon themselves the burdens of public office' (No. 75).

Leo XIII, encyclical *Diuturnum Illud (1881)*

'There is no reason why the Church should not approve of the chief power being held by one man or by more, provided only that it be just, and that it tend to the common advantage. Wherefore so long as justice be respected, the people are not hindered from choosing for themselves that form of government which suits best either their own disposition, or the institutions and customs of their ancestors' (No. 7).

11. Government, society and the individual

Social systems differ essentially in the way they consider the role of individuals, the society in which people live and how government should be run. The decisive question is this: how much room to manoeuvre does the state give to the individual and to social groups? We are touching on a fundamental problem of government and social life here. It is on this point that minds are often opposed to one another when it comes to making actual decisions in the political sphere.

In his 1944 Christmas broadcast Pope Pius XII, dealing with the subject of democracy, spoke of the state as 'an organic and organizing entity'. He regarded it as wrong to see the state as simply a sort of coagulation of all citizens in a certain territory, a mechanical accumulation of persons, in which the individual is on the one side and government and its institutions on the other. In reality, the individual never lives alone but is from birth tied into an intricate network of interpersonal relationships, social connections and institutional bodies. For this reason the liberal-individualistic as well as the totalitarian-collectivist view of the state have had to be rejected: from the outset the Church and Catholic social teaching have defended private rights and the right of individuals and organizations to live their own lives, in opposition to liberal and socialist conceptions. For a long time liberalism and socialism have ignored the importance of social groups and the associations they create.

The 'nightwatchman state'

There used to be a particular liberal approach to the concept of government that can fairly be described as a 'nightwatchman state'.

According to this, the state's most important duty was to look after the rights of the individual and render protection in much the same way as the nightwatchman of old protected the citizen from break-ins and robberies. For this reason the liberal state regarded with a certain scepticism the social formation of particular groups pursuing their own interests, because in its view the individual's rights and possibilities of personal development were being jeopardized. Such a state believed that maximum benefits to the individual and to society were assured only if everyone felt free from governmental compulsion and social pressures and so was able to fulfil his or her own destiny.

That is why the liberal state for many years denied the freedom of association, i.e., the right of individuals to form trade unions, and even refrained from state intervention when it became clear that the economic liberalism of the early capitalist era must lead, and indeed had led, to misery and hardship among the working classes.

The socialized person

On the other hand, the socialist concept was based on an extremely close association between people. It sought to establish a society in which people would live in a brotherly community of solidarity. The state, regarded in this way, should not just involve itself with economic life, but go well beyond that in pushing through equality between rich and poor and the various social groups, and in this way create real social harmony.

But to make this happen the state had to intervene extensively in every aspect of economic and business life and impose taxation systems to match. The socialist state, if it was to be consistent, had at the same time to become very comprehensive indeed, providing welfare services and general care for the whole community. This led to the curtailment of individual creativity and a loss of willingness to take responsibility. The 'socialized person' disappeared in the crowd.

The final stage was reached in the Marxist-Leninist state: there was no room left for free shaping of social and economic life. Everything was planned. All economic activity was determined by the government down to the last detail: the only organizations left were merely organs of the state. At the social and community level, the party shaped and controlled everything, even how leisure time and family life should be spent, and where and how to go on holiday through state-run organizations. And this revealed the true nature of the collectivist system: its totalitarianism. Because the human being will by nature rebel against such controls, the answer lay in communal and state dictatorship. Similar developments can be seen in many parts of the world even to this day.

Catholic social teaching

Faced with government authority, the Catholic Church speaks up on behalf of the individual and of small groups (such as the family) and associations of people. It is always vigilant for the free development of the individual personality, the strengthening of personal initiative and making personal responsibility more effective in both private life and in society. That is the only way to counter the dangerous trend towards thinking of the state as the all-provider and allowing the individual to become lost in the crowd.

Catholic social teaching regards the state as being built on a multitude of groups and associations which have a genuine right to a life of their own because, as a matter of history, they were there before the state was even thought of: one thinks of the family unit, social associations, local councils, corporations, the Church. To counter the constantly increasing burden of the state and the bureaucratization of public life, it is urgently necessary to strengthen intermediate social and state organizations and to have powers delegated to them as much as is practicable or possible, and also to delegate powers to non-governmental and private organizations.

The ideal is to have a many-faceted society with a great number of people all having responsibility of one kind or another; a society which gives each individual, group and association plenty of room for development; and which ultimately spreads the burden of decision-making to as many individuals and levels of society as possible.

This is highly effective in countering mass thinking and the manipulation of that mass. The individual enjoys the greatest possible freedom of self-development. And the threat of the abuse of power by the government and its organs comes up against a rigid barrier. In such a society citizens' initiatives also have a definite place – as long as they serve the general interest and not their own.

Subsidiarity and the state

To run successfully the kind of multi-faceted society described above, the principle of subsidiarity is of great importance. The principle of subsidiarity is one of the most important structural laws of a free society and democratic government. The state and other authoritative institutions should subordinate their task of giving help to the possibility of self-help by smaller groups and only intervene when those smaller groups are unable to cope from their own resources. Government should never take on any kind of activity that can more successfully be carried out by a group at lower level. The encyclical *Quadragesimo Anno* (No. 79) says: 'That which can be achieved by the individual human being with his own powers and by his own action should not be taken away from him and transferred to the community'. In this way government should be relieved of burdens so that it can the more effectively do those things which are its proper function.

This principle of subsidiarity is a cardinal principle of Catholic social teaching. It implies the rejection of every kind of collectivism and state omnicompetence.

Opinions are divided today on this fundamental issue. It concerns defending the right to personal development; that is, the possession of individual rights, independence and autonomy. It concerns, furthermore, the protection of smaller social groups against great and powerful organizations and, above all, against the state (e.g., in defence of the family and the rights of parents).

This principle of subsidiarity is not a one-way street with no-entry signs against the ubiquity of state power, however. It also imposes on the individual and the smaller group the obligation not to run to the state at the first opportunity, but to see first how their own capacities and opportunities can be effectively utilized – even at the cost, where necessary, to the individual of some sacrifice.

A common responsibility

Effective democracy depends on the active co-operation and shared responsibility of all its citizens. The more responsibility is given over to the government and its institutions, the fewer will be the democratic possibilities for exercising influence and shaping things the way individual people want. Democracy in the true sense of the word means that the responsibility for the community rests with every individual citizen and with all the people together. The mentality of 'spongers' who want to live at the community's expense without contributing anything themselves is not just anti-social but thoroughly undemocratic.

It is generally held that the state is responsible for looking after the public welfare, as the supreme protector and the guarantor of the interests of the community. Yet we should not leave this responsibility with the state alone. In our bureaucratic mass communities, that would inevitably lead to the omnipresent 'nanny state' which leaves no room for personal responsibility. Effective democracy depends on individual citizens responsibly directing their desires and interests towards the common good and actively working for the goals of the community. Times of crisis, particularly, always show how important responsible co-operation among all those involved can be. Issues that come to mind include environmental protection, reducing unemployment and many more.

What the Church says

Paul VI, encyclical *Octogesima Adveniens*

'Political power, which is the natural and necessary link for ensuring the cohesion of the social body, must have as its aim the achievement of the common good. While respecting the legitimate liberties of individuals, families and subsidiary groups, it acts in such a way as to create effectively and for the well-being of all, the conditions required for attaining man's true and complete good, including his spiritual end. It acts within the limits of its competence which can vary from people to people and from country to country.

It always intervenes with care for justice and with devotion to the common good, for which it holds final responsibility. It does not, for all that, deprive individuals and intermediate bodies of the field of activity and responsibility which are proper to them and which lead them to collaborate in the attainment of this common good. In fact, "the true aim of all social activity should be to help individual members of the social body but never to destroy or absorb them" ' (No. 46).

12. The duties of government

The nature of government is determined by the tasks entrusted to it. There is no dispute that its first duty is to act as supreme guardian of the common good. Differences of interpretation arise from where the emphasis is placed, and that depends largely on whether a government's responsibilities are narrowly or widely defined. Growth of the omnicompetent and totalitarian state has been stimulated in the past, not just by the absolutist but also by the socialist-collectivist state, and even in our own day by bureaucratic mass democracy.

What is the proper task of government? What are its *indispensable* functions? Throughout the ages, governments have tackled the greatest possible variety of tasks, including those well beyond their capabilities. We have to question the roles with which a government seeks to justify its authority and even its very existence, because there are certain things that only it can do and that are essential for a stable and peaceful society. Connected with such doubts is the criticism of the modern bureaucratic state and its tendency to regard itself as responsible for everything and to run every aspect of life in the community. In totalitarian, fascist and communist states the same happens – and ideology is taken as the justification.

Integration

Any state encompasses the community of all the people living in a certain territory. There are, of course, multi-national states, but history has shown and continues to show that as a rule they are always having to deal with new internal tensions and conflicts. The existence of a state depends on the people living within its borders feeling they belong together and hence constitute a natural community. In most cases this means ethnic affinity. When it comes to executing its functions, the state is first of all the visible expression of the society over which it has authority and the outward sign of common beliefs arising from a common heritage, people joined together by a common fate. It draws all these various people and communities and societies together and integrates the wide variety of their communal activities in the interests of the general welfare of the whole people.

The state is therefore more than just a mere instrument. It is the expression of a country's fate. Individuals will identify with the state because they are at home in it, because they feel an emotional attachment to the country, its people and its history. While Germans have specifically German difficulties in this, the same is not the case abroad, as is shown in the attitude of the English and the French to their flags or their national anthems. A nation that has no such self-awareness has given up and has no future.

The common good

All schools of political thought and social theory agree that the state is the supreme guardian and guarantor of the common good. It draws together the various social groups and activities and guides them in line with the shared goals of its society so that they are mutually enriched and strengthened and serve the entire community.

If it does not – and this applies to our complex modern societies and also to every other community – divergent interest groups will break the ties, and so the state needs authority and the power to back up its authority, including powers of compulsion. It would be quite a wrong interpretation of its duties if the state, because of its responsibility for the welfare of all, were to deprive individuals of responsibility, try to meet all personal needs from its own resources and so become a 'nanny state'. In general the state has only to provide the necessary framework to permit the individual, the family and social groups to be able to maintain themselves from their own resources and attain the goals they have set themselves.

Does this governmental duty include ensuring the spiritual salvation of the individual? The modern pluralistic state is compelled to adopt a neutral position towards different religious convictions: its powers are confined to life as it is lived on this earth. The state has no transcendental powers, no authority in the spiritual sphere, but as humanity is from birth destined for God – the human person is a being open to the transcendent – it is also a matter for the state to ensure that the citizens have all the opportunities they need to realize their own religious well-being, each according to his or her own convictions. And the contention that 'religion is a private affair' does not absolve the state from that obligation.

Internal security

The government's duty to ensure internal peace and safeguard security inside state borders springs directly from the need to protect the general welfare. The state has to draw together diverging groups and direct the pressures of individual sectors of the community within definite parameters towards attaining common goals.

Ensuring tranquillity inside the nation means that there must be an effective system of justice which guarantees the peaceful solution of arguments and conflicts: *iustitia fundamentum regnorum*. An independent and incorruptible judiciary is indispensable for social and communal peace: much of the poverty in the developing countries is directly attributable to widespread corruption and an unreliable system of justice.

The state also has to protect the life and liberty of the individual and to safeguard property – a difficult task sometimes for the police and law enforcement agencies. It is right that these should be subject to controls and open to criticism, but at the same time it is essential that they are given full public support if they are to carry out their difficult duties in the public interest.

Internal security depends on the government having a monopoly of force. Terrorism is not merely an attack on the state and the social order, it endangers the security of the judicial system and the existence of peace in the community. If the individual or if any particular group resorts to violence to gain its ends, peaceful existence becomes impossible and the law of the jungle will prevail. The idea of passive resistance, which is advocated and practised in some circles, is therefore also open to question: after all, resistance *is* resistance, and equal rights should *mean* equal rights. If every group were to resort to such means to attain its ends society would fall apart.

External security

The next basic duty of the state, and indeed a classic function of government, is to protect the citizen from external threat. This used to be accepted as utterly self-evident, but today it lies at the centre of all sorts of socio-political arguments. This fierce controversy is an expression of despair.

People have been made to feel insecure by the completely new situation created by the technical and scientific developments of recent decades. Old and tried strategies are failing, hitherto available defences seem powerless in the face of the new technical facilities, and established ethical rules seem little enough reason for moral approval of what might happen in a modern war; so resort to the new weapon systems appears questionable.

That argument begins with the condemnation of modern terrorism and its methods of fighting. Terrorists engage in acts of war: should they be fought by traditional means or should government call in the military? It is a difficult question, and impossible to evade if the state is not to leave the population helpless in the face of terrorism.

It is not possible to consider here the morality of nuclear and other weapons of mass destruction. The same applies to the current debate about conscientious objectors. Whatever the point of view, the basic truth cannot be avoided that a nation unwilling to defend itself has lost its spirit and has no future.

Social security

Another governmental responsibility today is establishing social and economic security; people cannot create these by themselves in an industrialized society. This duty includes making sure that the economy can function properly, job places are safeguarded and that there are adequate provisions for illness and accident insurance and social care. This responsibility, however, is controlled by the principle of subsidiarity: the government cannot act by itself, nor indeed is it the primary mover.

In the economic field in a free society, the state should set parameters in the socio-economic area, and then leave the economic forces to themselves and let managements and unions settle matters between them. A market economy cannot do without essential governmental direction in, for instance, business and labour policies.

To run the economy is not the government's real job: the exceptions may occur in developing countries. But there is always the danger that the state takes over more and more of the economy and so brings in state control by the back door. Special attention must be paid to this: neither a state-planned economy nor an omnicompetent welfare state are ideals of Catholic social teaching.

Anyone supporting a free society must support a free economy, and anyone who wants people to be free, responsible and mature should leave them free to make their own arrangements for their welfare; to do otherwise would in the course of time make them lazy and sap their determination to exercise responsibility, to be ready to make sacrifices and to make their own way.

The role of culture

No one can deny that government also bears responsibility for a community's culture, but again it has to be shared and does not arise from the state in the first instance. Only free communal forces can establish the development and growth of culture: to have it regulated by the state would be diametrically opposed to the very spirit of a free democratic society. The government must be there to support those free forces and give them the necessary equipment and facilities where needed. It should also be there in case individual cultural enterprises encounter difficulties. One particular field that is rightly passing more and more into government care is the maintenance of cathedrals, castles and ancient monuments, part of the nation's cultural heritage, simply because this is beyond private resources.

Schooling and education, however, are sore points. The modern state tends not only to take over control in this field but to decide what should be taught and to stamp a 'worldly' outlook on the content. Recently there has been irresponsible and undemocratic interference with the wishes and preferences of parents, independent organizations and Churches. Denominational schools have been put under the most systematic pressure and even abolished on the pretext of expanding equality of opportunity and providing a better education all round, leaving the way open for politically oriented schools to take the place of denominational schools. The socio-political aims of the Enlightenment are still too much with us, largely determining the course of education and training.

What the Church says

German Bishops' Conference, *The Tasks and Limits of State Authority (1953)*

'There are duties of government for which it is uniquely or primarily fitted. These are above all protection and security against dangers from abroad, and maintaining and guaranteeing a proper system of order based on justice at home. Peace, safety and order are the basic preconditions for a thriving and continuous community life, forming the foundations for the common good, and these the government must provide. First and foremost is the state regulation of order, a state based on justice, even though its duties do not end there. *Iustitia fundamentum regnorum*: justice is the foundation of the state. To maintain security and order the state has been given powers, but within the framework of justice and in the service of those aims which government has set itself.

'Beyond that there is a wide field of social and cultural duties in the exercise of which the state has to share with others. Carrying them out is primarily the function of individuals and groups in society. It is for the state to promote such activities and to a certain extent watch over them, without taking them over itself. It must intervene in such areas only, and take charge as a stimulator and representative only, if those responsible cannot do so satisfactorily and the interests of the community demand it.'

13. The limits of state power

Every theory of statecraft examines the limits of state power, to what extent government is in general terms bound by the law and by legislation, and beyond that to the controls over government and its institutions. Catholic teaching has developed its own basic rules, which go back to biblical and early Christian times. The closely connected question of the right of resistance to state power will not be considered here, however.

No picture of Catholic social teaching and its view of government would be complete if it did not consider the limits of state power. Christian tradition has always stood up firmly for state authority and its theological justification in what God wanted for the creation, but it has at all times just as firmly pointed out to the state and its rulers what they can and cannot do. That was particularly true for the Middle Ages and the close connection that then existed between spiritual and temporal power. At that time, the issue was not what to preach to princes or what code they should uphold; the frequent clashes between Church and state, between Pope and Emperor were not concerned merely with claims to worldly power. Behind all these medieval disputes about the supremacy of spiritual over temporal power was the politico-ethical attempt to bind the Emperor and worldly power to the law and judgment seat of God. The Emperor was subject to God's law just like everyone else.

Absolute state power rejected

The Church always condemns any state's claim to absolute power, regardless of where or in what form it is made. The despots of modern times and their claims to absolute power have never been accepted by the Church even if the ruler that has emerged is a Catholic. That applies also to the absolutist Church leaderships which placed the churches under state administration and control, and with similar consistency rulers' claims to responsibility for everything have been rejected in other fields as well. The identification of the ruler with the state (Louis XIV: *L'État c'est moi*) is just as irreconcilable with Catholic social teaching as the idea that the state's power is total and limitless.

The claim to absolutism by socialist-fascist states has been more radical even than that of the absolute despotisms of the past, but in whatever form it appears (whether a military dictatorship either of the right or left, whether it is socialist or national fascist) the totalitarian state cannot be reconciled with the principles of Catholic social teaching. Such governments are out to control completely all economic, social and political activities and to regulate and regiment them through their institutions even including the privacy of family life if possible. Independent social groups and associations are systematically excluded and all independent action inside the community is suppressed. Even when it does not offend against the moral or divine law, the totalitarian fascist state contradicts the goal of a many-faceted society in which social and political responsibility is broadly spread on the basis of subsidiarity, and even small social groups and associations and their own right to exist enjoy priority given them by the state.

The same applies to the Marxist-Leninist state and its claim to absolute power. The Marxist 'dictatorship of the proletariat' perhaps may have meant for Karl Marx a real supremacy *of* the people in the democratic sense, but Lenin soon made it a dictatorship *over* the people. Taking the role of the proletariat was the party and 'the party is always right', which means that it claims to possess a 'higher knowledge' which makes it infallible. In the Marxist party dictatorships, the people and their social groups lose every right to existence beside or outside party doctrine and state totality. No one can have a private life outside party control, even if it concerns only social, cultural, religious or scientific matters. Those who do not subject themselves to party doctrine are automatically subject to prosecution as dissidents.

Divine law

Every state claim to absolute power contradicts the convictions of the Christian faith. The Christian accepts that any absolute claim to people and their lives belongs only to God. The ultimate and decisive standard for Christian life is the revealed divine law. All state power finds its boundaries set by that. 'We ought to obey God rather than men' (Acts 5:29) means that every exercise of governmental authority is subject to God's law, just as every human being is, and that the citizen must withdraw allegiance to the state when it no longer obeys that law. There is a Christian right of resistance to the state when it goes against the will of God.

'We ought to obey God rather than men' gives Christians nothing to quibble about. Even so, there are certain problems. If we start with the interpretation of the scriptures and the revelation of divine law, one has to ask on what issue a pluralistic state can give a binding decision according to the Bible, when there would not be one forthcoming that is acceptable to all denominations and religious groups. And in many instances there are religious convictions other than those of Christians to be considered. And even if all religious groups were convinced of the existence of divine law, it would not always be easy to reach an agreed interpretation that would therefore be binding on our legislators. For instance, in the abortion law debate, opinions still differ considerably.

Another considerable difference concerns the question as to what extent a religious law can be made binding on a pluralistic society. When it involves the religious convictions of a particular denomination, the state cannot enact a law binding on everyone. Government must take into account the religious opinions of minorities. The divine law and a free conscience are the highest court that can ultimately limit state authority: they set limits the state dare not cross if it is not to lose its democratic and Christian legitimacy.

Natural law

In a pluralistic society the natural law, i.e., the general natural moral law, offers fair and equal foundations generally recognized by people of all persuasions. This law is binding on the state and the legislation emanating from it – that much is generally accepted. Laws offending against general moral convictions cannot bind the conscience of the citizen.

Yet here, too, there are problems similar to those encountered when considering interpretation of divine law, except that here they are even bigger: what authority can give an interpretation of the natural moral law that is universally acceptable? There is no dispute over principles when considering issues such as starting a war of aggression, but very much of a problem when it comes to concrete application of the natural moral law to particular situations. Let us consider for a moment the issue of property. How far must the legal system protect property? Does this law apply also to private ownership of the means of production? And, to take matters a stage further, to what extent should the government engineer a redistribution of property by fiscal measures? These are matters that are always open to argument.

Then there is the controversy whether, and to what extent, the government can call on public opinion or the democratic majority when interpreting natural moral feelings. Yet in the meantime the Universal Declaration of Human Rights has established a certain generally binding standard of moral convictions. Now it is generally accepted that the natural rights of human beings are the compelling norm for every government and every state authority.

Social groups' right to exist

When considering the limits of state power, we should not ignore Catholic social teaching's view that independent social groups and associations have a right to exist. Such groups place no inherent curbs on the state so far as the specific demands of the moral code are concerned. Enough has already been said, however, about the particular religious or ideological convictions of individual social groups and the respect to be accorded to minorities, but it is necessary to consider the issue of the institution of social groups as such.

Governmental administration, the organs that constitute the state authority and enable government to exercise responsibility in matters affecting communal and economic life, all have limits imposed on them by the individual right to exist of social groups and organizations.

Under the principle of subsidiarity, government should not act in those areas where individual or group strength can do what has to be done from their own resources. The powers of government only *begin* where the strength and resources of individuals, and their groups and institutions, cannot act. Which leaves us with the proven principle: the state bears the highest responsibility, but is not responsible for everything. And that is also a fair interpretation of the principle of subsidiarity when one looks at the state and its competence in competition with individual groups' right to exist.

What the Church says

John XXIII, encyclical *Pacem in Terris*

'Governmental authority, therefore, is a postulate of the moral order and derives from God. Consequently, laws and decrees passed in contravention of the moral order, and hence of the divine will, can have no binding force in conscience, since "it is right to obey God rather than men." Indeed, the passing of such laws undermines the very nature of authority and results in shameful abuse' (No. 51).

German Bishops' Conference, *The Tasks and Limits of State Authority (1953)*

'The state is intended to be the protector and guardian of the common good. For that reason all that happens in government has to serve that purpose. It is this task that gives it power by the will of God. From this task, too, its authority derives its limits. The state is not a means in itself, but the highest service to the common good. The individual and the smaller organizations which have set themselves up in free association inside the larger community of the state should not be restricted or oppressed in their development by state action; on the contrary, they should through the state discover better possibilities for their own development.'

14. The Pluralistic Society

Political realities today are largely shaped by a pluralistic view of the world. The fact that in our society individuals and groups hold widely differing views on life and religion demands from the individual and also from government a way of going about things that will ensure peace in society. In the pluralistic state a general consensus in the community about what constitutes the basis of communal living is no longer automatic: in contrast to earlier times, finding such a consensus itself becomes a social problem and can test the democratic state to breaking point.

Today we no longer live in a community that is to all intents and purposes closed when it comes to religion or ideology. The Catholic Church, and even the Christian faith itself, have to compete with other religions and philosophies. Because society is pluralistic the government has to take up a neutral stance towards the different opinion groups. However, it is necessary to speak out when the government has to tolerate something that in the eyes of the Church and the Christian faith contradicts the truth of the gospel. For a long time the Church reserved its position or indeed rejected entirely the liberal pluralistic society, but how does the Church judge it today? Does the Church take note in a positive way? What conclusions does the Church draw for its understanding of itself in this society?

Pluralism in society

People in Europe have lived in ideologically compact societies right down to our own day, societies marked by unifying religious convictions. On the basis of a common faith, social and political life could attain a large degree of harmony untouched by religious and philosophical conflicts. In both religious and community life, it was of equal importance that the ways of conducting relationships, moral standards and people's personal convictions were, broadly speaking, the same for everyone and that, therefore, there was no need to resort to conflict in the religious, communal or even private domain. Even the Reformation did not alter that. The Treaty of Westphalia of 1648 which ended the Thirty Years' War set the boundaries of the denominational areas and in fact they have hardly changed since then. And even in areas where Catholics and Protestants lived together under either Catholic or Protestant rulers, private and communal life was shaped by a common Christian faith and shared moral convictions.

It was the rise of the industrial society that sparked fundamental change. Another major factor was the rise of modern means of travel: railways, cars, aircraft. The old denominational borders have been swept away and are hardly of any consequence. Today we live in a pluralistic secular society with the widest possible variety of life-styles and convictions, competing religious and philosophical beliefs and a broadly-conceived ethical liberalism and, in some cases indeed, even nihilism.

A formal concept

For many people today pluralism is in itself a high, even the highest moral value. In this generally recognized pluralism they see the attainment of a truly free society in which all people can live their lives according to their own consciences and personal convictions without being forced into anything at all either by the state, the community or religious norms. Pluralism has itself become an article of faith.

There has been, however, a certain sense of disenchantment, a growing awareness that pluralism, taken in itself, has no positive value. Certainly the fact that it has engendered attitudes enabling us all to live peaceably together has not been valued highly enough; but pluralism itself does nothing to bind people together: it is not an integrating force. On the contrary, the more pluralism we have in social beliefs and the way we should conduct ourselves towards one another, the more the forces holding society together are split.

Pluralism does not possess inherent value but is, rather, a formal entity. It means openness towards differing life-styles and competing value judgments, and by virtue of this it builds up social and

248

individual freedom, yet every society needs a common basis, shared convictions about essential values. There has to be something that binds people together, otherwise life in community will ultimately become impossible. That this has not happened yet is due to the fact that, at least so far, we have evidently been living on a common basis of Christian faith and Christian values.

Perhaps we have lived for too long on the achievements of the past: now that our faith has increasingly been eroded, we are in danger of having too small a base. We can hardly make a joint stand today on major issues facing our society, let alone matters in everyday life. Internal conflicts are becoming more bitter. The readiness to use force to attain one's goals has grown dangerously. Terrorism is only the tip of the iceberg. Where will it all end? Can we believe, without giving the matter another thought, that our pluralistic society will continue to work, when the bonds that keep us together are being steadily weakened?

A basis of common values

The fact that pluralism contains in itself no integrating force whatever is becoming daily more obvious when we see the violent conflicts in society. The basis of common value judgments and attitudes has become narrower and narrower, so that we have to ask how long it will be before it ceases to function altogether as the binding force in communal and political life. Every society, every community, has a need for shared convictions to map out a common road and define the things that need doing and the way to do them. When there are no directions, everything comes to a halt.

It would be disastrous to believe that the demolition of all social and philosophical differences could provide a new basis by having a sort of lowest common denominator which could provide values for all, for what kind of values they be? One has only to look at the so-called basic values of modern democracy: liberty, equality, fraternity. No one should be fooled by such a splendid façade: there are no common beliefs and convictions behind it. The French revolutionary of 1789 and his communist counterpart of 1917, the liberal, the socialist, the Marxist, today's Christian, each and every one of them has understood these concepts quite differently, for the very reason that for a long time there has been no shared acceptance of what they stand for.

What gives cause for alarm, therefore, is not the further destruction of moral and religious values still being so vigorously pursued today, but the difficulty in giving one's life a consistent shape when there are so many differing values. If everyone were to admit to being tolerant over social and philosophical issues, it would be possible to shape a new common basis out of values and convictions as they are expressed in everyday life. No one can get away from responsibility for a moral and religious basis of values, not even the government. The neutral democratic state cannot itself set values but it can and must do all in its power to protect and strengthen them, or it will be reduced merely to having the ideology of a 'night-watchman state'.

The Church and pluralism today

The Church accepts pluralism as a fact of contemporary life. It has again explained its attitude clearly in the Second Vatican Council. Starting out from the view of itself as the pilgrimage of the people of God towards final attainment of truth and peace, it wants to share with human beings and society the quest for justice and peace. The Church knows that it is not of this world and that it cannot attain its goals by worldly means, but it regards itself as everyone's ally and as a negotiating party in today's pluralistic society, which it would like to serve with its potential and its gifts wherever possible. In solidarity with society, the Church wants to fight together with the people of our time for the realization of human rights, social justice and social peace. Church and society come together in this quest (*Gaudium et Spes*, No. 39, 26).

In the Council the Church confesses to social tolerance as a condition for people to live together in prosperity in a pluralistic society, yet it should never lose sight of the fact that, because of its purpose, it is also a sign of contradiction. If its willingness to work for solidarity with people and promote social co-operation were to lead to its compromising with the spirit of the times, the spirit of a secularized world, it would lose its power to be the salt of the earth and the light of the world.

What the Church says

German Bishops' Conference, *The Church in Today's Plural-istic Society and the Democratic State*

'We see around us ever more clearly that pluralism in itself possesses no integrating power. It needs active effort towards unity. This is a responsibility that belongs to everyone. The right kind of social policy gives general recognition of guaranteed constitutional rights, the necessary support and a clear expression of communal goals' (No. 18).

'It would be disastrous to conclude from modern pluralism that all differences must be done away with and that in public life only general opinions should be tolerated. Who would be able to guarantee that finally there would not be the constraints of a unitary world outlook and a power-political totalitarianism? Not infrequently in the Federal Republic of Germany, neutralist and levelling moves hide behind the slogan of "deconfessionalization" ' (No. 23).

'Both the religious and the worldly pluralistic communities need mutual recognition of common values if they are not to stoop to inconclusive wrangling. As has already been said, experience has shown that there can be no absolute pluralism and that pluralism as such cannot be the basis for peaceful and harmonious life among individuals and associations' (No. 25).

15. The state's neutrality on ideologies

Having a government that remains neutral when it comes to ideologies is one of the basic preconditions for peaceful and prosperous community life in a pluralistic society. The effects and the problems such a stance poses for government and society from the viewpoint of Catholic social teaching are analysed in what follows. It is a question that affects the religious convictions of individuals and therefore a settlement that is satisfactory to all concerned is of great importance.

Today's pluralistic state must remain neutral concerning the various views of religion and ideologies and the organizations that put them forward. The Churches cannot be an exception to this, even if they cannot be denied a special position deriving from their particular significance in the life of the community. Government neutrality concerning ways of looking at the world is not questioned today, particularly with regard to the need for order in peaceful co-existence among people, but even so its practical application can create tensions. It is never quite clear what effect the upholding of neutrality in the state and state institutions has on the various fields of social policy. One might ask just where are the sensitive areas.

Religious freedom

Freedom of religion is essential for harmonious living in a pluralistic society. The Catholic Church, which wanted to open itself out to pluralism in society at the Second Vatican Council, could not evade the problems involved. In *Dignitatis Humanae*, its declaration on religious freedom, it not only committed itself to such freedom but based it on the dignity of the human being and the essential nature of the act of faith.

Religious freedom is a human right based on the personal value of the individual and human freedom. This dignity is infringed when people are forced to act against the dictates of conscience, and no one should be prevented from living according to his or her religious convictions. Apart from this being based on grounds of humanity, freedom of religion is rooted also in the nature of faith itself. This theological justification derives from the freedom of grace: God does not want to force anyone into accepting faith. It is part of Church teaching that the human being accepts God's offer voluntarily and that no one 'should be forced into acceptance of faith against his will' (*Dignitatis Humanae*, No. 10).

The human right to this freedom, affirmed at the Council, should not be used as an argument against the Church itself or for exclusion of the Church and the religious life from the public arena. It would be a misunderstanding of this freedom and of social pluralism if, in the name of doing away with denominational and religious differences, some kind of unitary ideology were to be put in its place as a common basis for life in the community. Every religion has points in which the adherent believes in the true sense of the word, but a 'deconfessionalized' church or religion would be something where there are no such points and where there is no religious force left. This levelled-out world view would sterilize life in the community because it would no longer provide society with such stimuli.

The argument that 'religion is a private matter' has also to be rejected if it implies that religion should confine itself solely to private life. That would ill serve the community, for pluralistic democracy derives its own strength from the various groups in the community playing an active part in it and helping to build up moral, cultural and political life. Where would we get a thriving and stimulating communal ethos if it were not to spring from the various social groups, in particular those that are religious or have some other definite ideology? Sometimes there are even arguments about religious freedom itself simply to reduce the influence of the Churches and the freedom to speak one's mind and express one's faith.

The neutrality of the state

The right to religious freedom proclaimed in all human rights declarations means that the state must exercise strict neutrality in religious and ideological questions. There is neither the call for it to take sides in such issues, nor the power for it to do so according to its constitution.

Even so, the government cannot abdicate all responsibility. Religion *is* a private matter, but only insofar as each individual has to act according to the dictates of conscience. Religion becomes a very public matter when it comes to government creating for people the necessary conditions for publicly practising it. This obligation arises not just out of the human right to religious freedom but out of the duty to promote public welfare, the common good, because the religious quest is given to people from birth and to a large extent the well-being of the individual and the entire community depends upon how they follow it.

This brings us to the sensitive field of education. The modern state shows a fashionable weakness for pursuing a policy on education and training that smoothes over all differences of ideology. This is largely a legacy of the liberalism of the Enlightenment and its attitude to religion. There is no such thing as an education or a culture that is 'neutral' in the real meaning of the word. It is popular now to make fun of the Churches and accuse them of advocating religious 'indoctrination' in schools, but seeing to what extent their influence in the entire education system has been forced out, it would be better to draw attention to the alienation that now exists in all fields of instruction and the way ideologies have been fostered there. The space left vacant by the Churches has been taken over by groups building their own ideological bastions. Their progress through the entire education field is very clear to see.

Basic moral values

If government is compelled to take a neutral attitude to beliefs, and it has no powers in that field anyway, who is to take care of the ethos of the community? We have already established that pluralism is in itself not an integrating force and cannot inculcate values, but no society can survive in the long run if it has no basic moral values; the divisive forces of pluralism would gain the upper hand, would create constant conflicts without being able to settle them satisfactorily.

It is therefore up to the organizations in society to provide moral values, above all up to the Churches. It is the state that takes its values and moral convictions from the community, not the other way round. The Churches, the associations with various ideological standpoints, and all other such forces in the community, are in the front line. And because basic issues are involved the government cannot be indifferent to them. Just as we must give a clear 'yes' to the state's neutrality, so we must also say a clear 'no' to its indifference to the various world views. The state ought to support the organizations that speak up for these as much as it can. In fact, in a pluralistic society the government has more responsibility in this field than in other societies because that very pluralism is one of the main reasons why common values and convictions have disappeared.

The tremendous development in science and technology has given a new dimension to this quest for basic moral values. It has to be asked whether moral strength in the community is going to be equal to the challenge in issues such as human reproduction, genetic engineering and nuclear energy.

Does the people's sovereignty extend to the moral field?

If the state is to exercise its neutrality properly, should it be absolved from any duty to set standards? Should it stand aside, for instance, if all shades of opinion are ironed out in the cause of pluralism, which would lead automatically to ethical and religious levelling? This kind of approach is often enough advocated by militant nihilists, themselves not over-endowed with tolerance, who would like to see a militant nihilism take the place of positive religion.

Were the state indeed to be stripped of all power and responsibility in this field it would really have nothing left to do but act as the executor of the so-called popular will. But then the question must be asked whether it should obey every dictate of the people regardless? In response to this difficulty some have held the view in the debate on basic values that the Churches and social organizations alone bear the responsibility for all moral values in the community.

Is there actually some kind of 'people's sovereignty' in the field of ethics? Can matters such as truth, or good and evil, be decided by a majority vote? What would happen if the majority were to vote in favour of something which is clearly morally indefensible? True, politicians also have freedom of conscience and so do public administrators; but has not the government in some cases a power and responsibility of its own? Just as, according to universal opinion today, those having responsibilities during the Third Reich could not fall back on the commands of the Führer or the will of the German people, modern government and those who act in its name cannot rely simply on the will of the people democratically expressed. You cannot vote on truth. Humanity would fall into the moral abyss very quickly if government always took the line of least resistance and yielded in every case to the expression of the popular will.

What the Church says

German Bishops' Conference, *The Church in Today's Pluralistic Society and the Democratic State*

'The state is obliged to adopt a neutral attitude in religious and ideological matters. It has no competence to pass judgement on the validity of such convictions. This is above all true in the field of education. The idea that there can be education which is suspended above every kind of belief emanates from an ideological liberalism in no way recognized by all sections of a pluralistic society. Every kind of education depends on moral value judgments. It would contradict both pluralism and the unity it desires, if free decisions on a religious and moral education were to be excluded or curtailed by tactical manipulation or legislation' (No. 24).

16. The Church and Political Parties

Independent political parties are essential to the effective operation of a modern democratic system, and are important instruments for forging the democratic will and representing the various interests, hence the Church cannot remain aloof from them. Our post-war history has had its conflicts and all manner of reasons for irritation. How does the Church basically see its relationship to party democracy and the political parties?

Acceptance of democracy

In the Second Vatican Council the Church emphatically endorsed democracy as the form of government best suited to our time. The Council saw it as springing from people's own spirit and said: 'It is in full accord with human nature that juridical-political structures should, with ever better success and without any discrimination, afford all their citizens the chance to participate freely and actively in establishing the constitutional bases of a political community, governing the state, determining the scope and purpose of various institutions, and choosing leaders' (*Gaudium et Spes*, No. 75). In the Council's opinion democracy is for Christians a moral duty.

This fundamental acceptance is not just of democratic government but of active co-operation by Christians in democratic institutions. The Council urged 'recognition and respect' for the difficult and responsible work that politicians have to do and demanded ¯om Christians that they take part in political life actively and by holding responsible posts. 'Those with a talent for the difficult yet noble art of politics, or whose talents in this province can be developed, should prepare themselves for it and, forgetting their own convenience and material interests, they should engage in political activity' (ibid. No 75).

Active involvement in political life is a genuine role for lay people. Clerics, on the whole, should hold back: accepting public office involving the exercise of state power is generally forbidden in canon law (CIC can. 285, Par 3). The same applies to clerics taking part actively in political parties (CIC can. 287, Par 2).

It is mainly up to the lay members of the Church to turn Christian principles for political life into practical politics. And when they do this, as Pope John Paul II has ceaselessly made clear, they should align themselves not with one ideology or another but with the real gospel message – the only determining yardstick for Christians – and with Catholic social teaching. These rules apply to priests throughout Europe and in all continents. One should therefore not misinterpret as some sort of chicanery the Church's sincere wish that prominent priests should withdraw from government responsibility in Nicaragua. How would public opinion in our own country react if Catholic priests were to take up government positions?

Relationships with the parties

The Church fully recognizes the indispensable role political parties play in the democratic state, and yet its relationship with parties has occasionally remained in question. As long ago as the 19th century, it proclaimed its unequivocal rejection of political and ideological liberalism, exactly as it has done with the ideologies of socialism and Marxism. Indeed, the history of Catholic social teaching is the history of critical disputation with individualistic liberalism and collectivist socialism. In seeking limits to the ideologies of liberalism and socialism, the Church has steered its own course on the basis of the scriptures and the Christian view of humanity and has charted that course in Catholic social teaching. Right up to the years after the Second World War, this has determined its attitudes to both liberal and socialist political parties.

When eventually the Second Vatican Council redefined its attitude to society, the way seemed clear to rethink the Church's attitude to political parties. There was a call for it to be neutral in the party-political sense. It was asked to cut its close links with the Christian parties, which grew up particularly after 1945, and maintain instead contact with all parties – but at a distance. Today the talk of being equidistant has vanished: the parties and their supporters have realized that the matter was not so simple. If co-operation with the Church is not to be one-sided, the parties should ask themselves to what extent they are prepared to include in their programmes the principles the Church stands for, and to what extent they are open to the Christian understanding of humanity and society.

It is not the Church that determines its relationship with the parties but the other way round. The Council made very clear its willingness to co-operate with all groups in society, but how close that can be is up to each party to decide according to its ideological and socio-political goals. In the meantime, there is less talk of getting rid of ideology in political and social life than of putting it back.

Christians in the parties

Christians are called on to take an active part in the political parties. It is the only way in which the gospel can take shape in the field of politics. If Catholic social teaching is to be effective it should be turned into practical politics by Christian men and women, but that does not mean that such co-operation should lead to the Church's social message being assimilated to the mood of the moment in such a way that the salt of the gospel should lose its savour. On the contrary, the programmes and practices of the parties should be tested against the yardstick of the gospel and Church social teaching.

Membership of a party does not absolve one from being critically watchful of what it and its representatives are doing. That applies in every party, but more so where the central points of its programme are at some distance from what the Church teaches. To remain silent then is to be guilty of an offence. It would be interpreted by the party and by public opinion as consent and can become an alibi for pursuing politics at variance with the gospel.

It is, furthermore, important for the political work of Christians that there should be shades of opinion within Catholic social teaching. There are few issues in which there is just one solution. Above all when it is a matter of the concrete application of socio-ethical principles, there are often several possibilities present.

Catholic social teaching ought not to be seen as a textbook with ready-made solutions for everything: it is constantly invigorated by facing up to new problems and new social, technical and ideological developments. As long as the Church has not officially pronounced on an issue, 'no one is permitted to identify the authority of the Church exclusively with his own opinion' (*Gaudium et Spes*, No. 43). To proclaim one's own opinion as the sole answer, as happens from time to time in the peace debate, and then to dismiss all dissenting views as contravening Christianity is unchristian.

Pastoral letters?

A delicate issue are the pastoral letters in which bishops regularly exhort the faithful to take part in elections and call for the support of those politicians who pledge themselves to putting Christian principles into political practice. No one can deny the bishops the right to have their say on matters of the moment and to exercise their political responsibility in the light of the faith. The parties cannot be denied their responsibility either. Just as in earlier days the Church exercised its political responsibility by reflecting on the authority and message of princes, it has to do just the same concerning those who bear the burden of office in today's democratic state. No one can deprive the Church of this right.

The question has to be asked, however, whether it is prudent for the Church to speak out on political and social issues just before elections. This can do great pastoral harm, and misunderstandings cannot be avoided: many will suspect that the pulpit is being used for party political purposes. It can safely be assumed that the faithful who regularly attend the liturgy have already made up their minds and that the bishops' exhortations would be superfluous. It would therefore probably be better and more effective if, apart from generally encouraging participation in elections, the Church and its bishops were to make their statements on current political issues well away from an election and so make them stand out more clearly and uncompromisingly. In any case, what happens regularly may happen too much: sometimes a little less achieves a lot more!

What the Church says

Second Vatican Council, Pastoral Constitution *Gaudium et Spes*

'Those with a talent for the difficult yet noble art of politics, or whose talents in this matter can be developed, should prepare themselves for it, and, forgetting their own convenience and material interests, they should engage in political activity. They must combat injustice and oppression, arbitrary domination and intolerance by individuals or political parties, and they must do so with integrity and wisdom. They must dedicate themselves to the welfare of all in a spirit of sincerity and fairness, of love and of the courage demanded by political life' (No. 75).

German Bishops' Conference, *The Church in Today's Pluralistic Society and the Democratic State*

'We Christians, today more than yesterday, must recognize the fundamental role of political parties and take up responsibility in them. However, we must always assess critically the programmes and operations of the parties and movements in central government, the states and the local councils, by their honest openness about fundamental beliefs regarding people and society, beliefs which are for us Christians the norm and a duty of conscience. The autonomy of earthly things to which the Council testified does not mean that Catholics can abandon their ultimate foundation and goal and create a world that conforms with the passing spirit of the times' (No. 51).

Postscript

Europe's political landscape has been completely changed since the crumbling of the Berlin Wall, that hated symbol of the division between East and West. This historic event has had its impact on the geo-political situation the world over and its full effect cannot yet be measured. The military-political blocs which determined political, cultural and economic development since the end of the Second World War are in a state of dissolution. The Iron Curtain, which passed like an invisible divide through humanity, is losing its contours. Marxism-communism, regarded for so long by some idealists in both East and West as the future road to paradise, has instead been exposed as a disastrous road to failure.

The signs of the times all point to a new understanding and to the end of the political and military potential for conflict. All over the world, it is beginning to dawn on people that the political and social problems of our time cannot be solved by conflict strategies but by overcoming divisions and through co-operation and solidarity. The word 'reconciliation' is on everyone's tongue from Europe to southern Africa, from Central America to Indo-China.

In this context, Latin American liberation theology has also lost some of its appeal. Those theologians who conceived of it as a Marxist-oriented theory of conflict indeed have served it ill. The way of violence has turned out to be a cul-de-sac. Violence provokes counter-violence and sets uncontrollable forces in motion. Countries like Colombia, Peru, El Salvador and Guatemala live permanently in a state of war, with countless victims. In such areas civil war has put a stop to any progress.

Real social and economic progress in freedom and self-determination is possible in the long run only when all social groups and forces, capital and labour, town and country – the latter particularly important in the developing countries – work together constructively. People do not want theories of conflict but designs for living that guarantee the co-operation of all sectors of society on the basis of social equality and a fair distribution of income. And it is this idea that has guided the Catholic social movement since its beginnings in the 19th century. That is also the basic thinking behind Catholic social teaching since Leo XIII published *Rerum Novarum*, the first social encyclical, in 1891. Ultimately that is one of the very real reasons why the concept of the social market economy is so successful. That and Catholic social teaching are both based on the concept of social partnership.

The social partnership theory rests on the assumption that capital and labour are factors of production of equal weight and moment. Co-operation in solidarity of all groups and sectors is indispensable for an effective free system of society. Catholic social teaching does not deny the conflict of economic interest between capital and labour, but it does not regard this as unbridgeable, as Marxism does. A social order that is free and based on justice has to draw up a legal framework in which employers and unions can negotiate their various interests in a fair way. The state has to create the basic conditions and see to it that the various, and to some extent conflicting, interests are directed towards the common good.

The world has been set moving by the policy of openness introduced by President Gorbachev. *Glasnost* and *perestroika* have set new signals. The train has set off and we do not know yet who are on the journey and how it will affect the travellers individually, but one thing is quite certain: the signs of the times point to understanding, the reduction of tensions, and the reconciliation of social and political opposites.

Ever since he took office Pope John Paul II has worked tirelessly and unwaveringly towards this goal. On his journeys to the Third World he has spoken frequently of the 'civilization of love' or the 'civilization of reconciliation', which are to overcome the 'civilization of death'. The 'civilization of love' is a formula he is fond of using to define the goal of a Christian reform of society. As he puts it, this vision gives shape to the co-operation of everyone in solidarity building a fair and peaceful world. It rejects every kind of violence and oppression and condemns the exploitation of, and discrimination against, anyone.

It was in this sense that on 3 February 1985 the Pope sent a letter of reconciliation to the people of the Peruvian Andes who have been suffering for decades from the bloody consequences of a guerrilla war. He called on his audience to work without using force for a return to justice in economic and political relationships and to be 'architects of reconciliation' between the factions. He urged the Marxist-Maoist guerrilla 'Shining Path' movement to give up their 'ideology of hatred'. Violence would lead nowhere because it has no means to build, only to destroy. He pointed out that the Church recognizes people's right to fight for greater justice in social and political life, but it could not condone violence and terror as a means. The Christian must tread the path of understanding, dialogue and reconciliation.

In his development encyclical *Sollicitudo Rei Socialis* of 1987 the Pope continued this theme, pointing out that in the past the ideological clash between East and West had led to growing military confrontation. Tensions between the blocs had brought the world to the edge of a new global conflict and placed an extraordinary stumbling block in the way of Third World development.

The Church's social teaching was critical both of liberal capitalism and of collectivist Marxism (No. 21). The goal must be to overcome the contradictions and work towards worldwide solidarity between peoples and nations.

The Pope expressed his opposition to any form of violence and condemned every kind of terrorism (Nos. 10, 24). For the first time in any social encyclical, the system of free enterprise was defended against left-wing criticism. Where entrepreneurial initiative was held back and people's feeling of enterprise was impeded, their place would be taken by passivity, submission to bureaucracy and utter dependence on the state (No. 15). All this worked against the integral development of people and nations.

The Pope pointed out that Catholic social teaching must now more than ever face up to international problems and in particular take up the option of a 'preferential love' for the poor. He stressed that the particular tasks were reform of international trade relations, of world food and finance arrangements and the transfer of technology, and the evaluation of international organizations (No. 43). He felt that the reason for the lack of success in development effort up to now was not primarily economic. The one-sided technical and economic strategy still has to be overcome: the 'moral dimension' plays the decisive role. The 'structures of sin' to be found everywhere have their roots in personal sin: these 'structures' grow out of moral failures of relationship, and so it is a matter above all of moral renewal and changing people's attitudes, an utterly fundamental change of awareness that must lead to a new solidarity among human beings. Solidarity is an indispensable precondition for a peaceful solution of the development problems ahead.

The encyclical quoted Pope Pius XII's motto, 'Peace is the fruit of justice' (*Opus iustitae pax*), and added that with equal justice it could be said that peace is the fruit of solidarity (*Opus solidarietatis pax*) because the way to peace and development is solidarity (No. 39). In the words of John Paul II, the Church's many-layered mission can be summed up in its central task of seeking the reconciliation of the individual with God, with oneself, with other human beings and with the whole of creation (Apostolic Letter *Reconciliatio et Paenitentia*, No. 8 et seq.). The Church has been sent by the Lord to proclaim this reconciliation and to be itself the sacrament of reconciliation in the world. The Apostle Paul has written: 'in Christ God was reconciling the world to himself . . . and has entrusted to us the message of reconciliation' (II Cor. 5:19).

This reconciliation is the Church's true destiny and mission. Considering this, and the present world political situation, the question arises whether the development of a theory of reconciliation and, tied in with that, a practice of reconciliation, is not a primary task for Christian social teaching. A 'theology of reconciliation' seems to be the imperative of the hour.

Theodor Herr
Paderborn, 5 June 1990

Suggestions for Further Reading

Social teaching and witness: historical development

R.W. and A.J. Carlyle, *A History of Medieval Political Theory in the West*, Vol. 6, Part V, London 1927

E. Troeltsch, *The Social Teaching of the Christian Churches*, Vol. 1, London 1930

Christopher Dawson, *The Making of Europe*, London 1934

John Courtney Murray, *We hold these truths*, New York 1960

Cambridge Economic History of Europe, Vol. III, *Economic Organization and Policies of the Middle Ages*, Chapter VIII: *Conceptions of the Economy and Society*, C.U.P. 1965

John Gilchrist, *The Church and Economic Activity in the Middle Ages*, London 1969

Peter C. Phan, *Social Thought: Message of the Fathers of the Church*, Vol. 20, Wilmington Delaware 1984

Modern Teaching

J.Y. Calvez and J. Perrin, *The Church and Social Justice*, London 1964

Joseph Höffner, *Fundamentals of Christian Sociology*, Cork 1964

Richard L. Camp, *The Papal Ideology of Social Reform*, Leiden 1969

Michael Novak, *The Spirit of Democratic Capitalism*, San Francisco 1981

R. Charles with D. Maclaren, *The Social Teaching of Vatican II*, San Francisco and Oxford 1982

Donal Dorr, *Option for the Poor: One Hundred Years of Catholic Social Teaching*, Dublin 1988

G. Baum and R. Ellsberg, *The Logic of Solidarity*, New York 1989

John Coleman, *One Hundred Years of Catholic Social Teaching*, New York 1991

Index

268

269

261.8